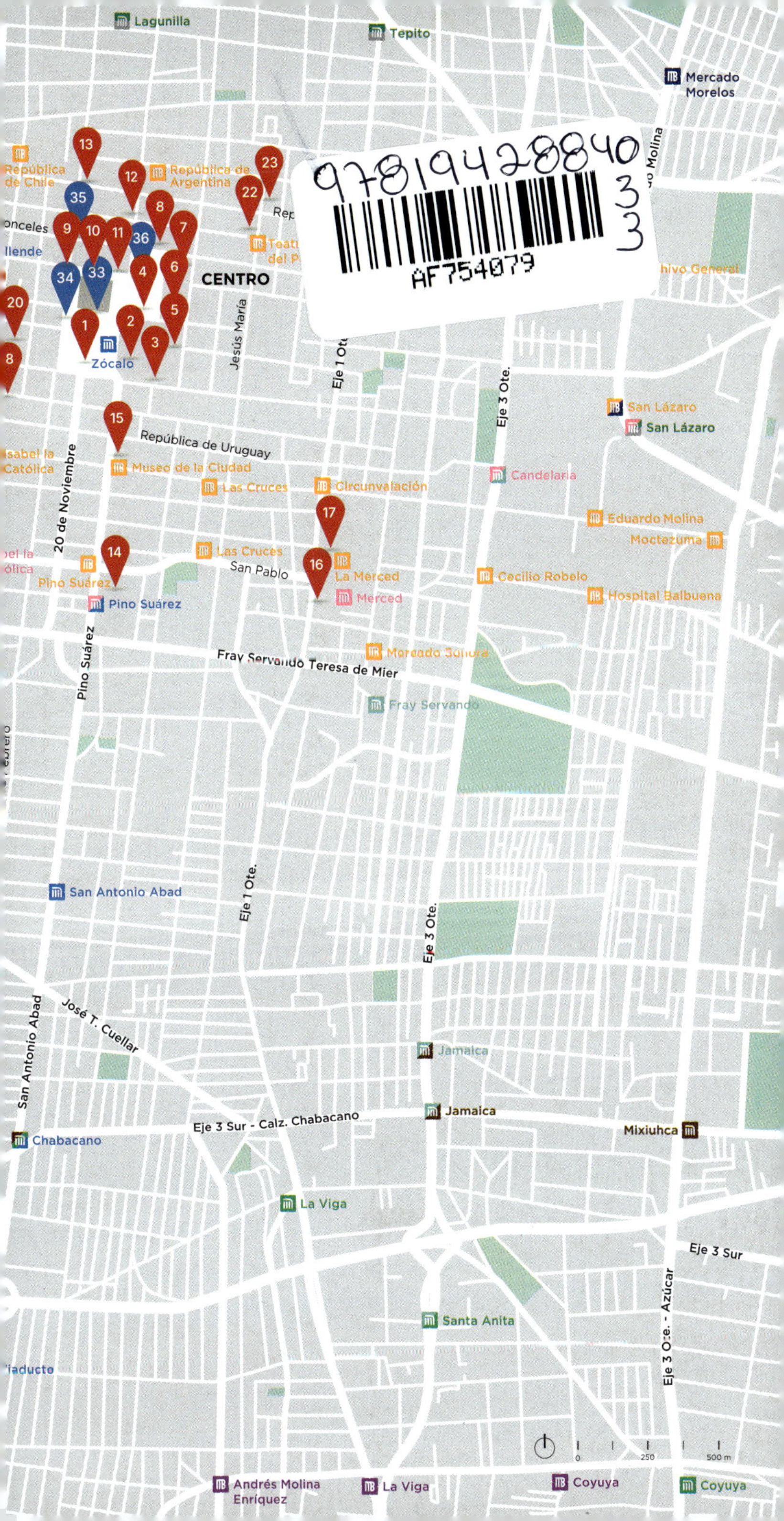
Lagunilla
Tepito
Mercado Morelos
República de Chile
República de Argentina
Rep
Teatro del P
Donceles
Allende
CENTRO
Jesús María
Zócalo
Eje 1 Ote.
Eje 3 Ote.
Molina
Archivo General
San Lázaro
San Lázaro
República de Uruguay
Isabel la Católica
Museo de la Ciudad
Las Cruces
Circunvalación
Candelaria
Eduardo Molina
Moctezuma
20 de Noviembre
Las Cruces
San Pablo
La Merced
Merced
Cecilio Robelo
Hospital Balbuena
Pino Suárez
Pino Suárez
Pino Suárez
Fray Servando Teresa de Mier
Mercado Sonora
Fray Servando
San Antonio Abad
Eje 1 Ote.
Eje 3 Ote.
José T. Cuellar
San Antonio Abad
Jamaica
Jamaica
Eje 3 Sur - Calz. Chabacano
Chabacano
Mixiuhca
La Viga
Eje 3 Sur
Santa Anita
Viaducto
Eje 3 Ote. - Azúcar
0
250
500 m
Andrés Molina Enríquez
La Viga
Coyuya
Coyuya
1
2
3
4
5
6
7
8
9
10
11
12
13
14
15
16
17
20
22
23
33
34
35
36

CDMX Guide
Seven Paths through
Mexico City
First edition, 2025

Miquel Adrià
Director

Ana Luz Valencia
Francisca Cortínez
Editorial Manager

Fátima Cabrera
Olmo Balam Juárez
Proofreading

Andrés Semo García
Assistant Editor

Estudio la fe ciega
Domingo Martínez
Yolanda Garibay
Design

Emiliano Muñoz
Map Production

Clara Marina Brugada Molina
Jefa de Gobierno de la Ciudad de México

Alejandra Frausto Guerrero
Secretaria de Turismo de la Ciudad de México

Carlos Martínez Velázquez
Director General del Fondo Mixto de Promoción Turística de la Ciudad de México

Jennie Shrem Serur
Directora General del Instituto de Promoción Turística de la Ciudad de México

Manuel Zepeda Mata
Director General de Equipamiento Turístico

Jorge Payró Pliego
Dirección de Administración FMPT

Jaime Alberto Rascón Mendizábal
Dirección de Promoción y Defensa de la Marca CDMX FMPT

Paula Ximena Molina Petrich
Dirección de Congresos y Convenciones FMPT

Andrés Semo García
Consultor

Doctor Lucio 181
Col. Doctores, 06720
Ciudad de México

arquine.com

CDMX
CIUDAD DE MÉXICO
CIUDAD DE MÉXICO
CAPITAL DE LA TRANSFORMACIÓN

CDMX®

CIUDAD DE MÉXICO

Guide

Seven Paths through Mexico City

Content

A City Like No Other

Mexico City is a living, deep, and diverse territory; a city of hope and memory. This city with a generous heart, a collective *yólotl*[1], is built through community, diversity, and resistance. In its neighborhoods and districts, in its plazas and public spaces, culture and tourism are understood as a right and as a form of care. Each of the routes represented in this guide reveals a broad spectrum of collectivity and authenticity.

From the Centro Histórico of Mexico City, a World Heritage Site where historic struggles and acts of resistance have taken place, to Chapultepec, a place where nature and culture are intricately intertwined, to Xochimilco, where the *chinampa* offers a living example of the resistance of Indigenous peoples and is also a World Heritage Site. Each of these paths reminds us that no transformation is possible without collective well-being.

This guide is an invitation to look closely, to listen to the voices of the past and the present, and to explore the Capital of Transformation.

Welcome to Mexico City, a city that reflects on itself, cares for itself, and grows from its people.

Alejandra Frausto Guerrero
Secretaria de Turismo de la Ciudad de México

[1] A female given name of Nahuatl origin meaning "heart."

In 2026, Mexico City is the urban center with the largest number of museums on the planet. We invite you to consult the city's agenda at the following site, where you will find all updated activities.

"As long as the world exists, the fame and glory of Mexico-Tenochtitlan will not end..." [1]

This guide presents the historical, cultural, and architectural richness of Mexico's capital city. Throughout the routes included in this book, you will discover a city built upon water and time, in an ancient basin that housed enormous lakes and witnessed one of humanity's most impressive construction feats: Tenochtitlan.

Today, Mexico City is the heir to that urban greatness, reflected in its buildings, streets, parks, gastronomy, and above all, in its people. Exploring it is, for both locals and visitors, an experience that surprises, delights the senses, and challenges traditional ideas about urbanism. It is a city where everyone is welcome, where activity never stops, but neither does the generosity and creativity of those of us who inhabit it.

This metropolis has hosted three World Cups and the 1968 Olympic Games. It has rebuilt itself after the earthquakes of 1957, 1985, and 2017, and survived the historic floods of the viceregal period. Furthermore, it is a city where gastronomy reaches extraordinary levels, where muralism found one of its most renowned artistic expressions in the world, and which safeguards an invaluable architectural, cultural, and social legacy, fundamental to understanding the course of human history.

Today, Mexico City is a symbol of modernity, technology, innovation, and sustainability. It is a pioneer in electromobility and distinguishes itself as an avant-garde capital that looks toward the future without forgetting its past.

Welcome, everyone, to the great Mexico City.

Carlos Martínez Velázquez
Director General del Fondo Mixto de Promoción Turística de la Ciudad de México

[1] Phrase attributed to the last *Huey Tlahtoani*, Cuauhtémoc.

How to Use This Guide

This guide brings together seven paths that cover more than 160 sites across Mexico City, from north to south, from the Basilica of Guadalupe to the Xochimilco boat landings. The selection includes temples, museums, buildings with particular significance in the city, as well as plazas and urban passages that, taken together, link the pre-Hispanic past with the contemporary vitality of the capital.

The texts and photographs—most of them produced especially for this edition—aim to present fragments from different periods that coexist within the same territory. Each path is named after the areas it crosses, although in many cases its route extends beyond those boundaries. The seven routes are distinguished by colors, with the sites numbered consecutively from 1 to 165. Organized into five maps, the first five routes appear in maps 1 and 2, from the northern limit of the itinerary at the Basilica of Guadalupe to Chapultepec, included in the fifth route; maps 3 and 4 correspond to the sixth route, and map number 5 shows the seventh and final route, in the south of Mexico City.

Each site is identified by the number that can be located on the map (A), followed by its name (B). This is followed by a block of practical information (C): address, nearby public transportation, the closest Ecobici station—when applicable—as well as opening hours and whether admission is free or paid, when this information is necessary for the visit. For sites with a website, a QR code (D) is included that links to it, providing additional useful information for the visitor. Each entry also includes a brief did-you-know fact (E) and a main text (F) that highlights the site's importance, characteristics, and history.

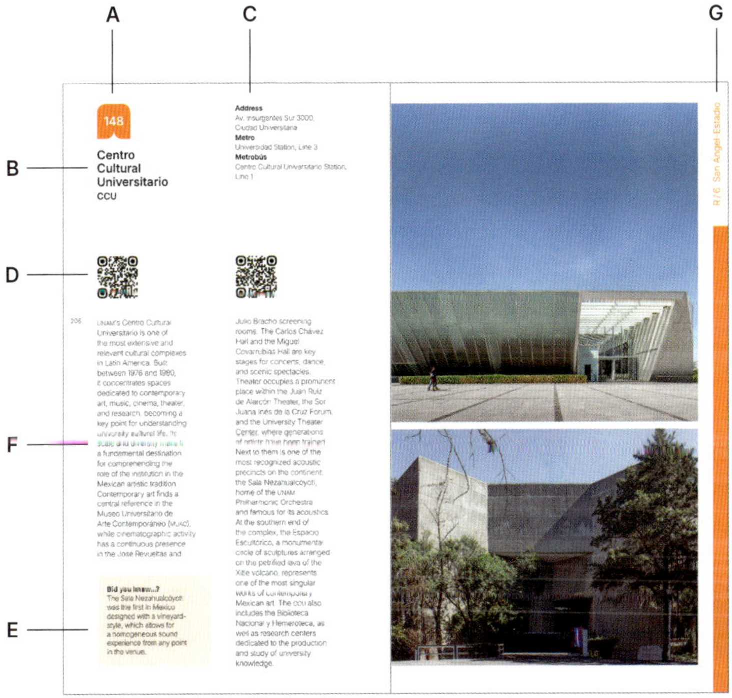

A Site number for map location

B Site name

C Practical information

D QR code linking to the website

E Interesting fact

F Body text

G Route name and color bar identifying each route

1

The Historic Center of Mexico City, known as Centro Histórico, is a territory shaped over centuries of urban, political, and social transformations. Across its 668 blocks—protected by UNESCO since 1987—vestiges of Tenochtitlan coexist with viceregal squares and temples, nineteenth century reforms, and interventions from the twentieth and twenty-first centuries.

Centro Histórico

The history of this space begins with the founding of Mexico-Tenochtitlan around 1325, on a small island in the middle of Lake Texcoco. The Mexica built a city on the water, mastering the lacustrine environment through *chinampas*, dikes, canals, and causeways. At the time of the conquest, Tenochtitlan had over 200,000 inhabitants and served as the political, military, and commercial center of a vast Mesoamerican empire.

The fall of the city in 1521 did not result in a new foundation from scratch, but rather the imposition of a new order over an existing urban fabric. Hernán Cortés and his Indigenous allies occupied the central spaces, destroyed temples and palaces and, following the layout drawn by Alonso García Bravo, established a Renaissance-inspired grid. The main square—today Plaza de la Constitución—was consolidated as the heart of viceregal power, surrounded by the government palace, the cathedral, and the residences of the elite.

Between 1521 and 1821, Mexico City became the administrative and symbolic center of New Spain. Temples, convents, hospitals, and hydraulic works were built; the city grew in population and social complexity, with Indigenous, *criollo* (creole), and caste neighborhoods. The square, today known as the Zócalo, was a constant stage for religious ceremonies, markets, floods, and civic festivities, where the viceregal order was enacted.

After independence, Mexico City maintained its centrality as the seat of government. The Reform laws transformed convents into civil buildings, while the Porfiriato introduced new avenues, streetcars, and French-inspired architecture at the cost of demolishing structures deemed obsolete.

In the twentieth century, urban expansion, the city's sudden growth, and the earthquakes of 1957 and 1985 contributed to the emergence of diverse architectural models and the replacement of historic structures with new urban developments, even as informal commerce grew and automobile use intensified. The designation of the Centro Histórico as a World Heritage Site in 1987 spurred restoration and pedestrianization efforts, and opened a new dialogue among conservation, tourism, everyday life, and urban development.

This first route explores the Centro Histórico as an urban nucleus where architecture and public squares condense seven centuries of history: there, an empire was founded, another was imposed, and successive projects of republic and nation were imagined.

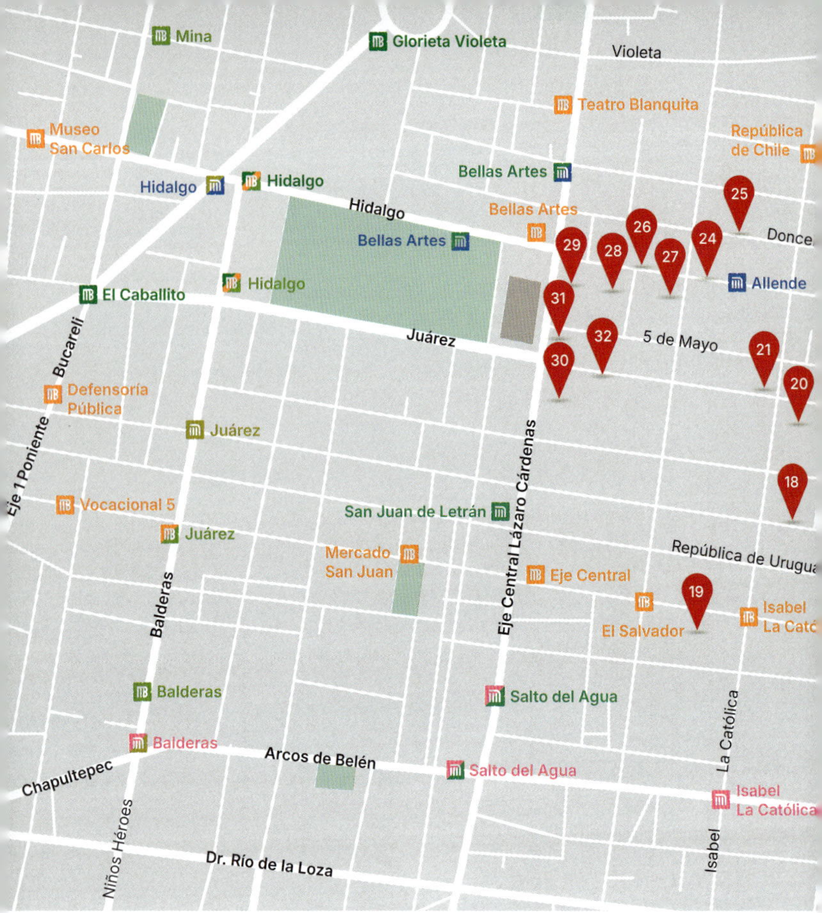

Route 1 / Centro Histórico

1 Zócalo / Plaza de la Constitución

2 Palacio Nacional

3 Mural *Epopeya del pueblo mexicano* at Palacio Nacional

4 Museo de la Secretaría de Hacienda y Crédito Público

5 Museo Nacional de las Culturas del Mundo

6 Ex Teresa Arte Actual

7 Palacio de la Autonomía Universitaria

8 Colegio de San Ildefonso

9 Hotel Catedral

10 Centro Cultural de España en México (CCEMx)

11 Museo de Sitio CCEMx-INAH

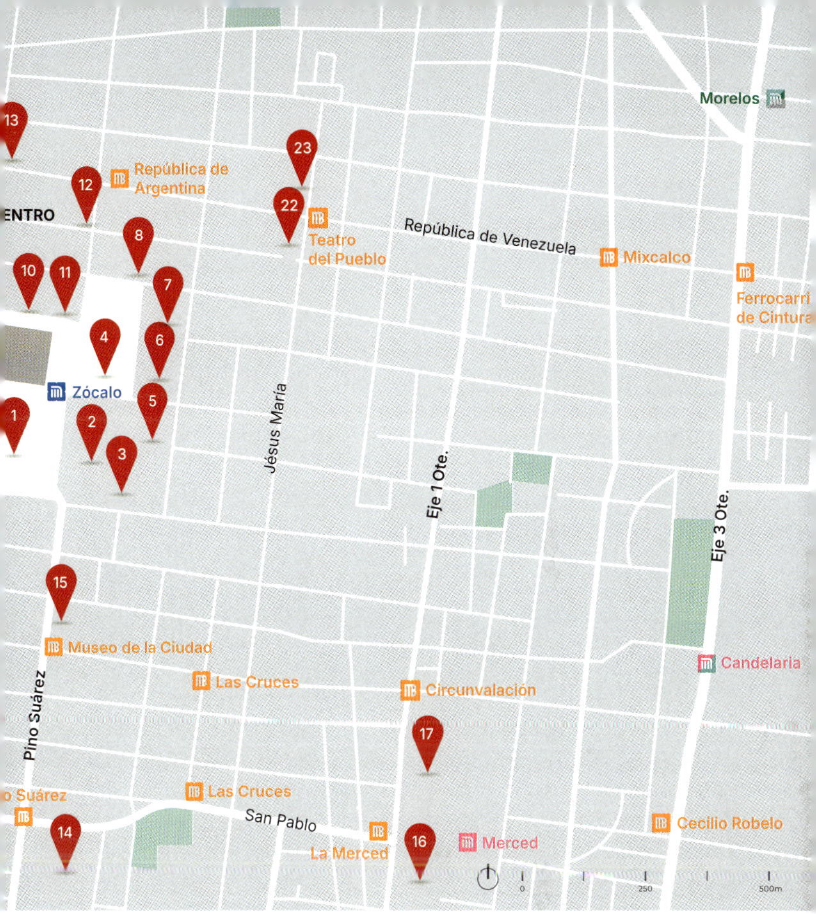

12 Museo Vivo del Muralismo

13 Palacio de la Escuela de Medicina

14 Adoratorio a Ehécatl

15 Museo de la Ciudad de México

16 Mercado de La Merced Nave Mayor

17 Mercado de Dulces y Flores de La Merced

18 Foro Valparaíso

19 Biblioteca Miguel Lerdo de Tejada

20 Museo del Estanquillo

21 Iglesia de La Profesa

22 Templo de Nuestra Señora de Loreto

23 Mercado Abelardo L. Rodríguez

24 Calle de Tacuba

25 Teatro de la Ciudad "Esperanza Iris"

26 Museo Nacional de Arte (MUNAL)

27 Museo Interactivo de Economía (MIDE)

28 Palacio de Minería

29 Palacio Postal

30 Torre Latinoamericana

31 Edificio y Museo Banco de México

32 Casa de los Condes de Orizaba

1

Zócalo / Plaza de la Constitución

Address
Plaza de la Constitución s/n, Col. Centro
Metro
Zócalo / Tenochtitlan Station, Line 2
Metrobús
20 de Noviembre Station, Museo de la Ciudad Station, República de Argentina Station, Line 4
Ecobici
CE-090

Did you know...?
The name Zócalo comes from the unfinished pedestal for a statue of Santa Anna in the nineteenth century; only the base remained, and the nickname endured.

At the political and symbolic center of Mexico City lies the Plaza de la Constitución, popularly known as the Zócalo. Before becoming a viceregal plaza, this square was the heart of Mexico-Tenochtitlan: the great esplanade facing the sacred precinct, where the roads of the *calpullis*, the causeways, and the ceremonies of power converged. After the conquest of 1521, a new grid layout was imposed upon the Mexica ruins. The main plaza was defined as the nucleus of viceregal power, surrounded by the Palacio Virreinal (today Palacio Nacional), the Catedral Metropolitana, and the City Hall. During the viceregal era, it functioned simultaneously as a market, a festive stage, and a place for royal proclamations, *autos de fe*, and religious processions. In the nineteenth and twentieth centuries, the Zócalo was transformed with gardens, streetcars, pavements, and urban reorganization, but maintained its centrality. From Porfirian parades to revolutionary rallies, from labor strikes to student demonstrations, the plaza consolidated itself as a forum for public life. Today, it remains the site of the Grito de Independencia festivities, massive protests, concerts, and cultural fairs. More than an square, it is an open space available for the demands, celebrations, and mourning of Mexican society.

2

Palacio Nacional

Address
Plaza de la Constitución s/n, Col. Centro

Metro
Zócalo / Tenochtitlan Station, Line 2

Metrobús
Museo de la Ciudad Station and República de Argentina Station, Line 4

Ecobici
CE-094

Hours
Tue-Sun 9:00 - 17:00 h

Entry
Free admission with prior registration

Did you know...?
After 135 years, in 2018, executive functions were fully relocated to the Palacio Nacional, which regained its status as the Presidential Residence.

The Palacio Nacional, located on the eastern side of the Zócalo, is one of the oldest and most significant buildings in Mexico City. Built on the site of Moctezuma's Palace, it was briefly the home of Hernán Cortés and, from 1562, became the seat of the viceroys of New Spain. For nearly three centuries, it was the administrative center of a vast viceregal territory. Its long facade of quarry and volcanic stone, spanning more than 200 m, responds to the sober language of viceregal civil architecture; the president enters through the Puerta Mariana for the Grito de Independencia. After independence, the building continued as the heart of political power and witnessed the Reform, the Porfiriato, the Revolution, and post-revolutionary governments. Today, in addition to serving as the seat of the Federal Executive Branch, much of the building functions as a museum, where visitors can encounter historical documents, courtyards, furnishings, and murals. Walking through it means entering centuries of national history and one of the clearest symbols of Mexico's power and transformation.

3

Mural *Epopeya del pueblo mexicano* at Palacio Nacional

Address
Plaza de la Constitución s/n, Col. Centro
Metro
Zócalo / Tenochtitlan Station, Line 2
Metrobús
Museo de la Ciudad Station and República de Argentina Station, Line 4
Ecobici
CE-094
Hours
Tue-Sun 9:00 - 17:00 h
Entry
Free admission with prior registration

Did you know...?
Rivera included discreet portraits of communist intellectuals and a tiny self-portrait, almost hidden, within the crowd representing the labor struggle.

The mural *Epopeya del pueblo mexicano* is one of Diego Rivera's masterpieces and one of the most complex visual narratives of modern art in México. Painted between 1929 and 1935 on the main staircase of the Palacio Nacional, the complex covers more than 450 m² and displays a monumental narrative that traverses, with a critical and epic sense, the history of the country from pre-Hispanic civilizations to the twentieth century. Rivera articulates this vision through densely populated scenes, political symbols, historical figures, and social allegories, generating a continuous visual cycle of struggle, resistance, and transformation. The mural is organized into three main bodies: in the center, the panorama of pre-Hispanic Mexico; to the right, the conquest, the viceregal period, and social movements; and to the left, modernity and the political tensions of revolutionary Mexico. Due to its scale and complexity, it is considered one of the most influential visual manifestos of muralism.

4

Museo de la Secretaría de Hacienda y Crédito Público

Did you know...?
The Pago en Especie program, created in 1957, allows artists to pay taxes with their work; promoted by Siqueiros, it allowed for the formation of one of the most important public collections of modern art in the country.

Address
Moneda 4, Col. Centro
Metro
Zócalo / Tenochtitlan Station, Line 2
Metrobús
República de Argentina Station, Line 4
Ecobici
CE-094
Hours
Tue-Sun 10:00 - 17:00 h

The Antiguo Palacio del Arzobispado is one of the oldest viceregal buildings in Mexico City. Located a few steps from the Zócalo, its origin dates back to the sixteenth century, when it was built as the residence of the second archbishop of Mexico, Fray Alonso de Montúfar, on ancient indigenous lands near the ceremonial precinct of Tenochtitlan. The current building is the result of successive construction stages between the sixteenth and eighteenth centuries. Its facade of volcanic and quarry stone preserves a sober Baroque portal with an episcopal coat of arms, while the interior features a central courtyard with arcades, stone staircases, and contemporary murals regarding the country's economic history. In 1957, the property passed to the SHCP, which dedicated it to cultural activities. Since 2002, it has housed the SHCP museum, Antiguo Palacio del Arzobispado, holding a collection of viceregal, modern, and contemporary art, largely acquired through the Pago en Especie program. Admission is free and offers an intimate visit, away from the downtown's bustle.

5

Museo Nacional de las Culturas del Mundo

Did you know...?
Before going to the Museo Nacional de Antropología, the Piedra del Sol was exhibited here, turning the building into Mexico's first great national museum.

Address
Moneda 13, Col. Centro
Metro
Zócalo / Tenochtitlan Station, Line 2
Metrobús
República de Argentina Station and Teatro del Pueblo Station, Line 4
Ecobici
CE-094
Hours
Tue-Sun 10:00 - 18:00 h
Entry
Paid admission

The building now occupied by the Museo Nacional de las Culturas del Mundo is one of the oldest institutional properties in the Centro Histórico. Designed in the sixteenth century to house the Casa de Moneda, it subsequently served as the headquarters of the Suprema Corte de Justicia and, from the late nineteenth century, the Museo Nacional de Arqueología, Historia y Etnografía. For decades, its courtyards of volcanic and quarry stone sheltered Mexico's main archaeological and ethnographic collections, including the Piedra del Sol. Declared a Historical Monument in 1931, the building entered a new stage when Rufino Tamayo painted in 1938 the mural *La Revolución* in the lobby. Following the inauguration of the Museo Nacional de Antropología in 1964, the venue redefined its vocation and was reopened on December 5 of the following year as the Museo Nacional de las Culturas del Mundo. Today, it houses permanent and temporary exhibitions on Asia, Africa, Europe, and America, as well as a specialized library and media center.

6

Ex Teresa Arte Actual

Address
Lic. Verdad 8, Col. Centro
Metro
Zócalo / Tenochtitlan Station, Line 2
Metrobús
República de Argentina Station, Line 4
Ecobici
CE-094
Hours
Tue-Sun 10:00 - 18:00 h

Did you know...?
Nineteenth-century travelers described this ex-convent as a symbol of female enclosure; its octagonal plan is unique in the city.

The former convent of Santa Teresa la Antigua, one of the most singular works of the late Novohispanic Baroque. Founded in 1616 by the order of the Discalced Carmelites, it was conceived as a space of strict enclosure for women of the Creole elite. The current building is the result of reconstruction following the earthquakes of 1711; the church, with an uncommon octagonal plan, was completed around 1813 under the direction of architect Cristóbal Rodríguez de Híjar. Its elliptical dome, the play of light in the drum, and the marble altarpiece make it an exceptional work within the city's Baroque panorama. After the Leyes de Reforma were promulgated, the convent was confiscated and served various uses until it was transferred to the Instituto Nacional de Bellas Artes y Literatura (INBAL) in 1993 as Ex Teresa Arte Actual, a space dedicated to experimentation in contemporary visual, sound, and performance arts.

7

Palacio de la Autonomía Universitaria

Address
Lic. Verdad 2, Col. Centro
Metro
Zócalo / Tenochtitlan Station, Line 2
Metrobús
República de Argentina Station and Teatro del Pueblo Station, Line 4
Ecobici
CE-094
Hours
Mon-Sun 10:00 - 18:00 h

Did you know...?
This building houses the largest archaeological window in Latin America.

The Palacio de la Autonomía occupies a historical building that has served multiple functions since the eighteenth century. Originally, it was part of the Colegio Máximo de San Pedro y San Pablo, a Jesuit institution dedicated to the training of priests and doctors of theology, and one of the most relevant educational centers of the viceroyalty. After the expulsion of the Jesuits in 1767, the property passed to the secular clergy and later to the State. During the nineteenth century and much of the twentieth, it housed various professional schools; from 1833 it was the seat of the Escuela de Odontología, a key element in the country's medical education. In 2004, the UNAM reclaimed and restored the building, naming it Palacio de la Autonomía in allusion to the university movement of 1929. Today, it houses exhibitions on the history of the university and its autonomy, and dental education, in addition to functioning as a venue for cultural activities, book launches, and academic conferences.

8

Colegio de San Ildefonso

Address
Justo Sierra 16, Col. Centro
Metro
Zócalo / Tenochtitlan Station, Line 2
Metrobús
República de Argentina Station, Line 4
Ecobici
CE-092
Hours
Tue-Sun 11:00 - 17:30 h
Entry
Paid admission, free on Sundays

Did you know...?
Inside the Colegio de San Ildefonso, in the Simón Bolívar Amphitheater, Diego Rivera created his first mural work, *La Creación*, in 1922.

The Antiguo Colegio de San Ildefonso is one of the most relevant cultural venues in the Centro Histórico. Founded in the sixteenth century by the Society of Jesus, it functioned for centuries as a college and seminary, and later as the headquarters of the Escuela Nacional Preparatoria. Its history is closely linked to the development of education in Mexico and to various political and cultural episodes of the nineteenth and twentieth centuries. The architecture of the complex combines viceregal and Neoclassical elements: wide courtyards, monumental staircases, and sober halls that refer to both the viceregal period and Porfirian modernization. San Ildefonso is especially known for its role in the origin of Mexican muralism. In the 1920s, Diego Rivera, José Clemente Orozco, and David Alfaro Siqueiros created some of their first murals here, driven by José Vasconcelos's educational project. These works, didactic and social in nature, articulate themes such as national identity, public education, and social justice. Currently, the venue functions as a museum and hosts temporary exhibitions, while preserving one of the most significant mural ensembles in the country.

9

Hotel Catedral

Address
Guatemala 16, Col. Centro
Metro
Allende Station, Line 2
Metrobús
República de Argentina Station, Line 4
Ecobici
CE-089

Did you know...?
The hotel's archaeological windows show Mexica structures *in situ*, allowing contemporary architecture and pre-Hispanic heritage to coexist under the same roof.

The Hotel Catedral is located a few steps from the Zócalo, just behind the Catedral Metropolitana, in one of the areas with the highest concentration of historical heritage in Mexico City's Center. Its sober architecture integrates with the viceregal surroundings, while its location makes it a strategic point for touring the ancient heart of Mexico-Tenochtitlan. The land was part of the Mexica sacred precinct, one of the most important ceremonial spaces of the pre-Hispanic city. Thanks to a collaboration with the Instituto Nacional de Antropología e Historia (INAH), on the ground floor of the hotel, one can observe—through archaeological windows—the pyramidal base dedicated to Ehécatl, god of the wind, and a fraction of the ancient ball game court. These vestiges belong to the same monumental complex as the Templo Mayor and allow for an understanding of the historical layering between the Mexica city and the current metropolis. The hotel also features a restaurant and a recently built tower, which offers privileged views of the Centro Histórico.

10

Centro Cultural de España en México (CCEMx)

Did you know...?
In the basement, vestiges of the Mexica *calmécac* can be seen, integrated into an archaeological window within the contemporary cultural center itself.

Address
República de Guatemala 18, Col. Centro
Metro
Allende Station, Line 2
Metrobús
República de Argentina Station, Line 4
Ecobici
CE-089
Hours
Tue-Sat 11:00 - 21:00 h
Sun 10:00 - 16:00 h

Behind the Catedral Metropolitana, almost hidden among viceregal buildings, the Centro Cultural de España en México is today one of the most active cultural hubs in the Centro Histórico. The building stands on part of the ancient *calmécac* of Mexico-Tenochtitlan, where the Mexica nobility was educated, and adds to those vestiges the walls of the Antiguo Palacio del Marqués del Apartado and a contemporary glass and steel extension open to the public in 2011. Rather than erasing layers, it places them in dialogue: pre-Hispanic past, viceregal layout, and current architecture coexist in a single complex. The CCEMx is part of the network of cultural centers of the AECID and, since 2002, has been dedicated to promoting contemporary culture, critical thinking, and human rights. Its programming includes exhibitions, concerts, cinema, workshops, and laboratories for youth and emerging creators, with free access and an emphasis on Ibero-American exchange.

11

Museo de Sitio
CCEMx-INAH

Address
República de Guatemala 18,
Col. Centro
Metro
Allende Station, Line 2
Metrobús
República de Argentina Station,
Line 4
Ecobici
CE-089
Hours
Tue-Sat 11:00 - 21:00 h
Sun 10:00 - 16:00 h
Entry
Free admission

Did you know...?
Excavations carried out before constructing the CCEMx revealed canals, floors, and walls associated with the *calmécac*, which allowed for the confirmation of its exact location within the ancient sacred precinct of Tenochtitlan.

On the site now occupied by the Centro Cultural de España, lie the vestiges of a space where contemporary life and Mexica memory overlap. The *calmécac* was the institution where the children of the Tenochca nobility were educated; they received instruction in astronomy, ritual music, writing, ceremonial discipline, and the principles guiding government and war. Priests, poets, and officials charged with guarding tradition and social order came from this center. Some vestiges of the ancient building can be observed in the courtyard of the current venue. This street corresponds to a stretch of the ancient Tlacopan causeway, one of the main roads of Tenochtitlan and a route connecting the sacred place with the west of the empire. This same causeway was used by Hernán Cortés during the so-called "Noche Triste". With the viceregal transformation, the layout adapted to the new city, but it preserves overlapping layers of indigenous and viceregal history. Today, it is a daily corridor for students and visitors, although the trace of the ancient ceremonial landscape persists beneath its surface.

12

Museo Vivo del Muralismo

Address
República de Argentina 28,
Col. Centro
Metro
Zócalo / Tenochtitlan Station,
Line 2
Metrobús
República de Argentina Station,
Line 4
Ecobici
CE-092
Hours
Wed-Mon 10:00 - 18:00 h
Entry
Free admission

Did you know...?
The museum preserves 289 original murals by more than ten artists; it is the most extensive mural collection in a single building.

Installed in the historic building of the Secretaría de Educación Pública, the Museo Vivo del Muralismo gathers more than 3,000 m² of restored mural painting. In its courtyards and halls—among them the Simón Bolívar Hall—works by Diego Rivera, David Alfaro Siqueiros, José Clemente Orozco, Jean Charlot, Roberto Montenegro, and other authors are preserved, distributed across various exhibition spaces. The circuit allows for the continuous observation of the development of Mexican muralism, from its post-revolutionary impulses to contemporary readings. The property, part of the complex declared World Heritage in the Centro Histórico, was fully restored between 2023 and 2024: stone was cleaned, gilding was reintegrated, and murals in historic offices, such as that of José Vasconcelos and the Ibero-American Hall, were rehabilitated. The museum incorporates a library, a children's room, and a multisensory space, offering guided tours, audio guides, and educational services.

13

Palacio de la Escuela de Medicina

Address
República de Brasil 33, Col. Centro
Metro
Allende Station, Line 2
Metrobús
República de Chile Station, Line 4
Ecobici
CE-262
Hours
Mon-Sun 9:00 - 18:00 h

Did you know...?
In more than three centuries of activity, the Inquisition in Mexico recorded around fifty formal executions, a figure much lower than popular perception suggests.

In the Plaza de Santo Domingo stands one of the most unsettling and significant buildings of the Centro Histórico: the Palacio de la Escuela de Medicina, the former headquarters of the Tribunal of the Holy Office. Built between 1732 and 1736 by architect Pedro de Arrieta, it features a facade of volcanic stone, frames of gray stone, and its famous beveled corner, designed to orient the building toward the plaza. For more than two centuries, it was the core of Novohispanic inquisitorial trials, featuring hearing rooms, dungeons, and reserved chambers. Following the abolition of the Inquisition in 1820, the property had various uses until becoming, in the nineteenth century, the seat of the Escuela de Medicina of the UNAM (Universidad Nacional Autónoma de México). Today, completely restored, it houses the Museo de la Medicina Mexicana, with rooms dedicated to pre-Hispanic practices, viceregal knowledge, scientific instruments, and twentieth-century medical advances.

14

Adoratorio a Ehécatl

Address
José María Pino Suárez,
Col. Centro

Metro
Pino Suárez Station, Lines 1 and 2

Metrobús
Pino Suárez Station, Line 4

Ecobici
CE-097

Hours
Mon-Fri 5:00 - 24:00 h
Sat 6:00 - 24:00 h
Sun 7:00 - 24:00 h

Entry
Paid (Metro fare)

Did you know...?
Pino Suárez metro station is the only one in the city's transport network with a pre-Hispanic platform visible from the surface.

At the intersection of Metro Lines 1 and 2 at Pino Suárez Station, one of the most singular examples of archaeology integrated into the contemporary city is preserved: the shrine dedicated to Ehécatl-Quetzalcóatl, the Mexica god of the wind. It was discovered in 1967 during the construction of the subway system, and a decision was made to preserve it *in situ*, incorporating it into the station's pedestrian flow. The circular base corresponds to the typology of Ehécatl temples, whose forms allude to the movement of air. This small sanctuary was part of the Zoquipan neighborhood, in the southern zone of Mexico-Tenochtitlan, and dates from the Late Postclassic period. Although surrounded by display cases, corridors, shops, and stairs, its presence recalls the physical layering between the Mexica city and the current metropolis. Its preservation set an early precedent in Latin America for permanently integrating a pre-Hispanic vestige within a modern public infrastructure. This station is located within the quadrant of the ancient city of Tenochtitlan.

15

Museo de la Ciudad de México

Address
José María Pino Suárez 30, Col. Centro
Metro
Pino Suárez Station, Lines 1 and 2
Metrobús
Pino Suárez Station, Line 4
Ecobici
CE-097
Hours
Tue-Sun 10:00 - 18:00 h
Entry
Paid admission

Did you know...?
At the corner of República del Salvador and Pino Suárez, there is a carved stone of pre-Hispanic origin.

The Museo de la Ciudad de México occupies the former Palacio de Los Condes de Santiago de Calimaya, one of the most outstanding Baroque residences of the eighteenth century, completed in 1779 by architect Francisco Antonio Guerrero y Torres. The museum offers a panoramic view of urban evolution from Mexico-Tenochtitlan to the contemporary city, through rooms dedicated to the pre-Hispanic, viceregal, nineteenth-century, and modern periods. Among its most distinctive spaces are the studio and music room of painter Joaquín Clausell, as well as the Jaime Torres Bodet Library, dedicated to urban memory. Its programming includes temporary exhibitions, workshops, concerts, and educational activities addressing themes such as identity, migration, and the environment. Inaugurated as a museum in 1964, the building was remodeled by Pedro Ramírez Vázquez, preserving original elements such as the shell fountain, friezes, and the family coat of arms rediscovered in the twentieth century.

16

Mercado de La Merced Nave Mayor

Address
Circunvalación s/n, Col. Centro
Metro
La Merced Station, Line 1
Metrobús
La Merced Station, Line 4
Ecobici
CE-097
Hours
Mon-Sat 5:30 - 18:00 h
Sun 5:30 - 14:00 h

Did you know...?
The area takes its name from the former La Merced convent, which was partially demolished after the Leyes de Reforma.

The Mercado de La Merced, and specifically its Nave Mayor (Main Hall), is one of the most extensive and complex commercial spaces in Mexico City. Located to the east of the Centro Histórico, in an area of exchange since viceroyalty times, it concentrates wholesale and popular trade in fruits, vegetables, seeds, flowers, and daily staples. The modern market was inaugurated in 1957, during the government of Adolfo Ruiz Cortines, as part of an urban modernization program. Its design, by architect Enrique del Moral, replaced the traditional *tianguis* and viceregal structures that had occupied the neighborhood since the nineteenth century. The Nave Mayor, with parabolic roofs and monumental dimensions, functioned for decades as the capital's main food distribution point, until the opening of the Central de Abasto in the 80's. The fire on December 24, 2019, damaged hundreds of stalls and triggered reconstruction projects. Today, La Merced remains a fundamental node for the city's popular and wholesale commerce.

17

Mercado de Dulces y Flores de La Merced

Address
Circunvalación s/n, Col. Centro
Metro
La Merced Station, Line 1
Metrobús
La Merced Station, Line 4
Ecobici
CE-097
Hours
Mon-Sun 8:30 - 18:00 h

Did you know...?
During the Day of the Dead season, La Merced concentrates the largest volume of *cempasúchil* and traditional sweets in the city, supplied by producer families of several generations.

Within the vast commercial complex of La Merced, two essential spaces for popular trade are found: Mercado de Dulces y Semillas, and Mercado de las Flores. Both were established in 1957 as part of the great project to modernize the city's supply system, although their activity dates back to much older traditions. The Mercado de Dulces y Semillas gathers *alegrías*, wafers, milk fudges, dried fruits, spices, and bulk products supplying both families and confectioners and merchants. During festivities, especially Day of the Dead, it becomes a key point for stocking altars. A few steps away, the Mercado de Flores begins activity before dawn, receiving shipments from Xochimilco, Guerrero, Atlixco, and other regions. Here, gladioli, tuberoses, marigolds (*cempasúchil*), and seasonal flowers are distributed, supplying florists, temples, and family celebrations. Together, both markets keep popular economy and agricultural traditions of the basin alive.

18

Foro Valparaíso

Address
Venustiano Carranza 60,
Col. Centro
Metro
Zócalo / Tenochtitlan Station,
Line 2
Metrobús
Isabel La Católica Station,
Line 4
Ecobici
CE-088
Hours
Wed-Sun 10:00 - 18:00 h
Entry
Free admission

Did you know...?
The palace preserves original frescoes and stands out for the more than 17-meter-long arch with no apparent support, the house's internal portals, and the double helical staircase.

Foro Valparaíso occupies one of the most outstanding Baroque civil buildings of New Spain: the Palacio de Los Condes de San Mateo de Valparaíso. Built between 1769 and 1772 as the residence of Don Miguel de Berrio y Zaldívar, the first Count of Valparaíso, it is a masterpiece by Francisco Antonio Guerrero y Torres, a central figure of Mexican civil Baroque. Its architecture combines *Chiluca* quarry and volcanic stone (*tezontle*) in a sober and monumental composition, topped by a portal with a central balcony supported by richly carved corbels. During the nineteenth century, it had various uses—residence, commerce, and public offices—until passing to the Banco Nacional de México in 1884. Following a extensive restoration, the property opened in 2021 as Foro Valparaíso, a museum space that articulates viceregal, modern, and contemporary art with historical documentation and original furniture. The visit highlights ornate halls, stone staircases, caste paintings, and current pieces in dialogue with eighteenth-century Creole memory.

19

Biblioteca Miguel Lerdo de Tejada

Address
República de El Salvador 48, Col. Centro
Metro
Isabel La Católica Station, Line 1
San Juan de Letrán Station, Line 8
Metrobús
El Salvador Station, Line 4
Ecobici
CE-102, CE-100

Did you know...?
Vlady's murals in this venue cover more than 2,000 m², one of the most extensive murals of the twentieth century in Mexico.

This nineteenth-century republican venue occupies the former Oratory of San Felipe Neri "La Profesa," transformed in 1929 into a civil space dedicated to public knowledge. Its architecture preserves the scale and solemnity of the original temple: a wide nave, high vault, frontal natural light, and dark wood shelves creating a disciplined and contemplative atmosphere. Among its central elements is the mural program by Vladímir Kibálchich, created between 1972 and 1982. These works, of great historical relevance, represent fundamental episodes of Mexican liberalism, the Reform, and the construction of the modern State. Their intense colors contrast with the serenity of the space and make use of the height of the former oratory to produce a vertical reading linking the religious past and secular thought. The venue also safeguards a documentary collection essential for political and financial research in the country, making it a key site for scholars and those interested in Mexican public history.

20

Museo del Estanquillo

Address
Isabel La Católica 26,
Col. Centro
Metro
Allende Station, Line 2
Metrobús
Teatro Blanquita Station and República de Chile Station, Line 4
Ecobici
CE-088
Hours
Wed-Mon 10:00 - 18:00 h
Entry
Free admission

Did you know...?
Carlos Monsiváis's collection includes more than 500 original political caricatures, many published in newspapers that disappeared in the twentieth century.

At the corner of Isabel la Católica and Madero Avenue, the Museo del Estanquillo occupies the old Porfirian building La Esmeralda, restored to house the personal collection of Carlos Monsiváis. Inaugurated in 2006, the museum safeguards more than 20,000 pieces reflecting the cultural and political life of Mexico: engravings, caricatures, photographs, models, books, and popular objects gathered with a critical and ironic gaze. The name "Estanquillo" alludes to the neighborhood shops where everything was sold, a metaphor for the diverse character of the collection.
As well as exhibiting valuable pieces, the museum proposes a visual reading of the country's modern history through everyday objects and printed materials. Its exhibitions address themes such as political satire, urban life, Golden Age cinema, and iconographies of power, with works by Posada, Álvarez Bravo, Vicente Rojo, or Gabriel Vargas. The venue also features a cafeteria, bookstore, auditorium, and a terrace with a view of the Centro Histórico.

21

Iglesia de La Profesa

Address
Isabel La Católica 21,
Col. Centro
Metro
Allende Station, Line 2
Metrobús
República de Chile Station
and Isabel La Católica Station,
Line 4
Ecobici
CE-088

Did you know...?
In the nineteenth century, around the so-called "Profesa Secreta", key support for monarchical projects took shape, from backing Agustín de Iturbide to the negotiations preceding the arrival of Maximilian.

In one of the oldest areas of the Center, this temple—popularly known as La Profesa—has been a religious and artistic landmark since the viceregal period. Its full name is Oratorio de San Felipe Neri, and its origin dates back to the late sixteenth century, when the Jesuits established a house of religious and missionary formation here. The current church was built between 1714 and 1720, after an earthquake damaged the original building. The design is attributed to Pedro de Arrieta, a prominent architect of the Novohispanic Baroque and author of the Palacio de la Inquisición and the Colegio de San Ildefonso. The facade, in volcanic and gray stone, combines Solomonic columns, niches, and reliefs in a sober composition. The interior preserves a main altarpiece of moderate Baroque style and richly decorated side altars. The Latin-cross plan, ornate vaults, and viceregal oil paintings—several attributed to Juan Correa and Cristóbal de Villalpando—make the temple a benchmark of Novohispanic sacred art. Today, it continues in liturgical use, and its sacristy, adapted as a gallery, safeguards a significant collection of religious painting.

22

Templo de Nuestra Señora de Loreto

Address
San Ildefonso 80,
Col. Centro
Metro
Zócalo / Tenochtitlan Station,
Line 2
Metrobús
Teatro del Pueblo Station,
Line 4
Ecobici
CE-092

Did you know...?
The tilt of the temple is perceptible upon entering: the floor is uneven and some columns appear displaced. Even so, the structure has withstood earthquakes thanks to several reinforcements.

Next to the old Colegio de San Gregorio stands one of the last Baroque temples of New Spain. The current church was built between 1805 and 1816 over the remains of a previous chapel, to serve the old neighborhood of Cuepopan, inhabited by indigenous and mestizo populations. The project was initiated by Rodríguez de Híjar, and its final appearance was defined by Manuel Tolsá. It features a Latin-cross plan and a dome over 30 m high situated on an octagonal drum, one of the most visible elements in the northern profile of the Centro Histórico. Built in volcanic and quarry stone, the complex combines features of the late Baroque with initial elements of Neoclassicism. The facade is sober, while the interior preserves side altarpieces, ample proportions in the transept, and viceregal oil paintings attributed to Juan Correa and Cristóbal de Villalpando. The weight of the dome caused subsidence starting in the nineteenth century, leading to several stabilization interventions, including a hidden metal reinforcement in the 80's. After the liberal Reform, it lost part of its heritage, and in the twentieth century, it was at risk of demolition. Today, it functions as a parish seat and is an architectural reference for its structural complexity.

23

Mercado Abelardo L. Rodríguez

Address
República de Venezuela 72, Col. Centro
Metro
Zócalo / Tenochtitlan Station, Line 2
Metrobús
Teatro del Pueblo Station, Line 4
Ecobici
CE-092

Did you know...?
The market's murals form the most extensive artistic ensemble ever created in a public supply building, integrating painting and sculpture into a single daily route.

This market is one of the most unique venues in the Centro Histórico: a popular supply space that, since 1934, has integrated early functionalist architecture with a notable mural program. Its layout occupies an entire city block and is organized through wide modules, high ceilings, and corridors that favor circulation, creating a sober architectural support that allows public art to take center stage. The murals, coordinated by Diego Rivera and executed by artists such as Pablo O'Higgins, Ramón Alva de la Canal, Ángel Bracho, Antonio Pujol, and sisters Marion and Grace Greenwood, cover walls and corridors with scenes of social criticism: agricultural work, labor exploitation, education, and the anti-fascist struggle. An exceptional element is the relief by Isamu Noguchi, an experimental piece introducing avant-garde languages within a popular market. Touring this space reveals how the post-revolutionary project integrated art and daily life, turning the market into a laboratory of social modernity.

24

Calle de Tacuba

Address
Tacuba, Col. Centro
Metro
Allende Station, Line 2
Metrobús
Bellas Artes Station, Line 4
Ecobici
CE-065, CE-089

Did you know...?
Remains of the original Mexica causeway subsist beneath Tacuba; archaeological studies have found sections of stakes and volcanic stone following the exact current layout.

Tacuba Street is one of the oldest and most symbolic routes in Mexico City. Its origin is found in the Mexica causeway that linked Tenochtitlan with Tlacopan, a ceremonial and political road that was also a commercial transit route and the stage for fundamental episodes, such as Cortés fleeing during the so-called Noche Triste. Today, Tacuba retains its historical character while articulating a series of emblematic buildings that reflect urban transformation: viceregal palaces, temples, nineteenth-century mansions, and cultural venues such as the Museo del Perfume (MUPE), the Palacio Postal, the Museo Nacional de Arte, and Plaza Manuel Tolsá. Its straight layout recalls the Mexica logic of connecting the directions of the world with the sacred precinct. Walking it is to traverse a sequence of historical layers where styles, memories, and contemporary uses coexist. Tacuba remains one of the liveliest routes in the Centro Histórico.

25

Teatro de la Ciudad "Esperanza Iris"

Address
Donceles 36, Col. Centro
Metro
Allende Station, Line 2
Metrobús
República de Chile Station, Line 4
Ecobici
CE-091

Did you know...?
The current curtain reproduces the original 1918 design, rescued during the restoration after one of the fires and reintegrated as a central piece of the auditorium.

The Teatro de la Ciudad "Esperanza Iris" is one of the most relevant scenic venues in the Centro Histórico. Open to the public in 1918 over the old Teatro Xicoténcatl, it was promoted by soprano Esperanza Iris, whose international prestige allowed the capital to be endowed with a theater comparable to great European venues. The building, designed by Federico Mariscal and Ignacio Capetillo-Servín, combines a monumental Neoclassical facade with an interior inspired by La Scala in Milan: a horseshoe-shaped auditorium, boxes, an orchestra pit, and a stage slope calculated to optimize acoustics. With a capacity for more than 1,300 spectators, the theater has hosted opera, zarzuela, dance, plays, and concerts for over a century. Following a fire in 1984, it underwent a comprehensive restoration that preserved its historical character and consolidated it as a current space for national and international performing arts.

26

Museo Nacional de Arte (MUNAL)

Did you know...?
Before becoming a museum, the building functioned as the Palacio de Comunicaciones y Obras Públicas. The iconic staircases, made of wrought iron, stand out for their decorative motifs inspired by organic forms such as acanthus leaves.

Address
Tacuba 8, Col. Centro
Metro
Bellas Artes Station, Lines 2 and 8
Metrobús
Bellas Artes Station, Line 4
Ecobici
CE-065
Hours
Tue-Sun 10:00 - 18:00 h
Entry
Paid admission, free on Sundays

This building—the work of Italian architect Silvio Contri and completed at the end of the Porfiriato—responds to an eclectic style combining Neoclassical influences with Baroque and Renaissance details, reflecting the modernizing and monumentalist impulse of Porfirio Díaz's regime.
It stands out for its interior architecture: marble staircases, stained glass, monumental columns, and a central dome illuminating the main patio. Outside, the plaza preceding it is presided over by the equestrian sculpture of Charles IV, known as *El Caballito*, created by Manuel Tolsá and considered one of the masterpieces of Novohispanic public art. Since 1982, the building has housed the Museo Nacional de Arte, whose permanent collection offers a chronological tour of more than four centuries of aesthetic production.
The exhibition is organized into three main sections: viceregal art, nineteenth-century art, and early twentieth-century art. In its halls, works by Cristóbal de Villalpando, Miguel Cabrera, Hermenegildo Bustos, José María Velasco, Saturnino Herrán, and other fundamental artists can be appreciated. The museum is also an active space for research, conservation, and dissemination.

27

Museo Interactivo de Economía (MIDE)

Did you know...?
Within the exhibition, visitors can explore the interest rate and observe how your choices affect inflation, growth, and macroeconomic stability in a few minutes.

Address
Tacuba 17, Col. Centro
Metro
Allende Station, Line 2
Metrobús
Teatro Blanquita Station, Line 4
Ecobici
CE-065
Hours
Tue-Sun 10:00 - 17:00 h
Entry
Paid admission

The Museo Interactivo de Economía, located in the former headquarters of the Convent of the Betlemitas, is one of the most innovative cultural spaces in the Centro Histórico. Inaugurated in 2006, it was the first museum in the world dedicated entirely to explain the functioning of the economy in an accessible and interactive way. Its rooms combine technology, simulators, tactile modules, and immersive experiences allowing for the understanding of concepts such as supply and demand, inflation, sustainability, international trade, and public policy. Housed in an eighteenth century building, is one of the city's late Baroque jewels. Its restoration respected walls of volcanic stone, original proportions, and the central courtyard, integrating these elements into the contemporary museographic design. The MIDE functions as a bridge between architectural heritage and economic education, allowing students, families, and professionals to experience economic complexity through simulated decisions and practical exercises.

28

Palacio de Minería

Address
Tacuba 5, Col. Centro
Metro
Bellas Artes Station, Lines 2 and 8
Metrobús
Bellas Artes Station, Line 4
Ecobici
CE-065
Hours
Wed-Sun 10:00 - 18:00 h
Entry
Paid admission, free on Sundays

Did you know...?
The Palacio de Minería was one of the first civil buildings in America drawn entirely with academic plans based on European treaties, which facilitated its study and graphic reproduction since the nineteenth century.

This building is one of the most representative works of Neoclassicism in Mexico City. It was built between 1797 and 1813 by architect Manuel Tolsá, a central figure of viceregal academic art and also responsible for the completion of the Catedral Metropolitana. Conceived as the headquarters of the Real Seminario de Minería, it responded to an Enlightenment project seeking to professionalize an activity key to the Novohispanic economy through training in mathematics, physics, and technical disciplines linked to metal extraction. The central courtyard, organized around semicircular arches on various levels, and the monumental staircase with curved stone ramps are considered today outstanding pieces of academic architecture from the late eighteenth century. After Independence, the property continued to be linked to engineering education and, until 1954, housed the Faculty of Engineering of the UNAM. Currently, it maintains its university and cultural vocation with exhibitions and conferences.

29

Palacio Postal

Address
Tacuba 1, Col. Centro
Metro
Bellas Artes Station, Lines 2 and 8
Metrobús
Bellas Artes Station, Line 4
Ecobici
CE-065
Hours
Tue-Sun 10:00 - 17:00 h
Entry
Free admission

At the corner of Tacuba and Eje Central stands one of the most singular buildings of the Centro Histórico, inaugurated in 1907 during the final years of the Porfiriato. It was conceived as the main headquarters of the national postal service in an era when mail represented modernity and territorial articulation. Beyond its function, the building stands out for its profusely ornamented architecture and the technical rigor with which it was built. The project was designed by Italian architect Adamo Boari, in collaboration with Mexican engineer Gonzalo Garita. The building combines Neo-Gothic references, Venetian details, staircases with an imperial air, and ornaments linked to European Modernism. This mixture is materialized with Carrara marble, wrought iron, gilded bronze, and artisanal stained glass. The facade, worked in white stone, displays winged lions, spiral columns, and balconies that project with lightness. The entrance leads to a wide lobby where the marble staircase with bronze railings stands out, one of the most recognizable elements of the property. Even today, it functions as a post office, making it possible to observe daily activity within historic walls. Over more than a century, the Palacio de Correos has withstood earthquakes, interventions, and changes in communication without losing its character. It has also hosted exhibitions, chamber concerts, and architectural tours allowing appreciation of its functional and aesthetic value.

Did you know...?
The structure of the palace is supported by a metal frame imported from the United States, which allowed for accelerated construction and gave it unusual resistance for the time, especially against subsequent earthquakes.

30

Torre Latinoamericana

Address
Eje Central Lázaro Cárdenas 2, Col. Centro
Metro
Bellas Artes Station, Lines 2 and 8
Metrobús
Bellas Artes Station, Line 4
Ecobici
CE-052
Hours
Observation deck
Mon-Sun 9:00 - 22:00 h
Entry
Paid admission for observation deck and museum

Inaugurated in 1956, the Torre Latinoamericana is located at the corner of Av. Francisco I. Madero and Eje Central. For several years it was the tallest building in Latin America and remains one of the most outstanding achievements of twentieth-century Mexican engineering. Beyond its height —182 m to the tip—it stood out for resolving the challenge of being built on the lacustrine subsoil of the Centro Histórico. Designed by architects Augusto H. Álvarez and Enrique León Parra and financed by the company La Latinoamericana, Seguros y Vida, it was the first skyscraper in the world in a high-seismicity zone with a deep foundation and a flexible steel structure supported by piles traversing the soft layers of the ancient lake of Mexico. Its good performance in the earthquakes of 1957, 1985, and 2017 confirmed the system's efficacy. During the 1950s and 1960s, it was consolidated as an emblem of modernity. The first levels housed offices, shops, and services, while the upper floors featured an observation deck, a museum, and a restaurant, offering a new way to experience the city from above. The observation deck, open to the public, remains as one of the best-known spots for admiring Mexico City, from Paseo de la Reforma and the Alameda Central to the Zócalo area. Although other buildings surpass it in height today, the Torre Latinoamericana retains its value as an architectural and technological landmark of the twentieth century.

Did you know...?
When the tower was built, its location was strategically chosen to visually terminate Av. Madero, the most modern commercial corridor at the time. Madero was the first pedestrian street in the Centro Histórico (pedestrianized in 2010), and its daily flow exceeds that of many main avenues.

6:16:24
6:16:24
LATINO SEGUROS

31

Edificio y Museo Banco de México

Address
5 de Mayo 2,
Col. Centro
Metro
Bellas Artes Station, Lines 2 and 8,
Allende Station, Line 2
Metrobús
Bellas Artes Station,
Line 4
Ecobici
CE-052
Hours
Tue-Sun 11:00 - 17:00 h
Entry
Free admission

Did you know...?
The building features steel armored doors manufactured in the United States and an underground ventilation system designed to withstand fires, in addition to preserving the original furniture of the boardroom from 1929.

Built between 1925 and 1928, and commissioned by the federal government, it was designed by architect Carlos Obregón Santacilia, with advice from engineer Manuel Ortiz Monasterio and collaboration from American architect Paul Philippe Cret. Since its inauguration, it has functioned as the operational headquarters of the Banco de México, conceived to project institutional solidity and financial modernity. The property is one of the first examples of institutional *art déco* in Mexico. Its steel structure is covered with *Chiluca* quarry stone and features ornamental details in bronze and marble. On the main portal, two winged female sculptures stand out, the work of Oliverio Martínez, representing security and economic firmness.
In 2021, the Museo Banco de México was inaugurated within the same building, following a restoration that allowed internal areas to be adapted without altering its financial operation. The museographic proposal addresses the central bank's role in the national economy—monetary policy, banknote issuance, inflation, and international reserves—and includes audiovisual material, historical documents, coins, and banknotes from different eras.

32

Casa de los Condes de Orizaba

Address
Av. Francisco I. Madero 4, Col. Centro
Metro
Bellas Artes Station, Lines 2 and 8
Metrobús
Bellas Artes Station, Line 4
Ecobici
CE-055
Hours
Mon-Sun 7:00 - 24:00 h

Did you know...?
The soda fountain maintains the style of the early twentieth century and still preserves part of its original furniture. José Clemente Orozco worked here on the murals that today form part of the restaurant tour.

This building, popularly known as Sanborns de los Azulejos, synthesizes commercial history and urban culture. The original construction dates from the sixteenth century, although it acquired its current form toward the end of the eighteenth century, when the family of the Count of the Valle de Orizaba remodeled it and covered it with blue and white Talavera tiles from Puebla, a gesture of ostentation in an era when cladding a house with ceramics was a sign of wealth.
Over time, it functioned as a manorial house, a warehouse, and a tenement. In 1919, it was acquired by brothers Walter and Frank Sanborn, who transformed it into their flagship establishment: a place to eat, drink coffee, and purchase pharmacy items, magazines, or gifts under one roof, a formula that was met with immediate success.
The interior preserves *art nouveau*-inspired stained glass, carved wood ceilings, wide staircases, and a mixture of Baroque and Porfirian elements. Among its best-known spaces is the hall housing the mural *Omnisciencia* (1925) by José Clemente Orozco, one of his first large-format works.

2

This route invites visitors to discover the historical essence of Mexico City, where cultural syncretism and Indigenous heritage intertwine to tell its story from the roots. Beginning at the emblematic Zócalo, facing the imposing Catedral Metropolitana, the route unfolds as a tribute to the city's foundation and evolution, linking its pre-Hispanic past with its contemporary urban character.

Catedral / Basílica

The Zócalo is a meeting point of traditions and eras, where the traces of the ancient Mexica civilization can still be felt in the remains of the Templo Mayor of Tenochtitlan. This temple, the spiritual and political heart of the pre-Hispanic world, was the *axis mundi* of Mexica society in ancient Tenochtitlan. Surrounding this square, several of the city's most significant buildings come into view: to the north, the Catedral Metropolitana, built over the course of three centuries; to the east, the Palacio Nacional—the seat of the executive branch—constructed atop the remains of Moctezuma's palace; to the south, the City Council and its twin structure; and to the west, the historic Merchants' Arcade, now home to various shops and hotels.

A short distance away, the remains of the *calmécac*—an educational center for the Indigenous nobility—reveal the importance that the original peoples placed on learning, writing, and the transmission of knowledge.

The route continues through the urban fabric of the Centro Histórico, where streets and squares reflect the memory of countless episodes. Each step through these streets reveals the layering of the present over a past filled with history and ancestral architecture.

A few steps to the north lies the well-known Lagunilla Market, which recalls a less visible past where objects and antiques gain new life through commercial exchange.

The route proceeds to Tlatelolco, a stoic site where the archaeological zone and the Templo de Santiago—birthplace of New Spanish scholarship and repository of codices—evoke the encounter between cultures. From there, the path leads to the former Pulque Customs House, now the Museo Indígena, and continues along Calzada de los Misterios until reaching the Basílica de Guadalupe. This sanctuary, a gathering place for millions of pilgrims each December, culminates the route at the convergence of history, faith, and tradition.

This route not only invites visitors to learn about the city, but to recognize the fusion of times and cultures that have shaped modern Mexico City. Along this path, it becomes evident how every street and every building safeguards a part of its history.

Lindavista
Hospital Infantil La Villa
De Los Misterios
Deportivo 18 de Marzo
Deportivo 18 de Marzo
46
Delegación Gustavo A. Madero
Eje Central Lázaro Cárdenas
Fortuna
Magdalena de las Salinas
Garrido
Euskaro
Euskaro
La Villa Basílica
Coltongo
Autobuses del Norte
Av. Talismán
Calzada Vallejo
Insurgentes Norte
Potrero
Potrero
Necaxa
Calzada de Guadalupe
Calz. de los Misterios
Cuitláhuac
Héroe de Nacozari
Eje 3 Norte (Cuitláhuac)
Excélsior
La Raza
La Raza
La Raza
Robles Domínguez
Paganini
Hospital la Raza
SANTA MARÍA INSURGENTES
45
Eje 1 Oriente - F.C. Hidalgo
Eje Central Lázaro Cárdenas
Circuito
Circuito
Misterios
Misterios
San Simón
Circuito Interior
Tolnáhuac
Manuel González
Mercado Beethoven
Tlatelolco
Tlatelolco
43
42
39
44
Peralvillo
TLATELOLCO
40
Eje 2 Norte - Canal del Norte
Ricardo Flores Magón
38
41
Tres Culturas
P. de la Reforma
MORELOS
Canal del Norte
Guerrero
SANTA MARÍA LA RIBERA
Glorieta Cuitláhuac
Guerrero
Guerrero
37
TEPITO
Garibaldi
Garibaldi y Lagunilla
Lagunilla
Tepito
Eje 3 Ote.
Glorieta Violeta
Mina
Violeta
Teatro Blanquita
35
Eje 1 Ote.
Morelos
Hidalgo
Bellas Artes
República de Chile
República de Argentina
Hidalgo
Hidalgo
Teatro del Pueblo
Ferrocarril de Cintura
Bellas Artes
Bellas Artes
36
Allende
Isabel La Católica
34
33
Donceles
Mixcalco
Hidalgo
Juárez
5 de Mayo
Archivo General
Balderas
Juárez
San Juan de Letrán
Zócalo
Jesús María
Mercado San Juan
CENTRO
0
250
500m
San Lázaro
Juárez
Eje Central
República de Uruguay

Route 2 / Catedral-Basílica

33

Catedral Metropolitana

Address
Plaza de la Constitución s/n, Col. Centro
Metro
Zócalo / Tenochtitlan Station, Line 2
Metrobús
República de Argentina Station, Line 4
Ecobici
CE-089
Hours
Mon-Sun 9:00 - 17:30 h

Located in the heart of the Centro Histórico, on the Plaza de la Constitución, the Catedral Metropolitana de la Asunción de la Santísima Virgen María occupies a main place within the limits of the ancient sacred precinct of Tenochtitlan. Its construction began in 1573 and concluded in 1813, which explains the coexistence of styles ranging from the Renaissance to the Baroque and the Neoclassical. It is the second cathedral of Mexico City. The first, built shortly after the fall of Tenochtitlan with materials from the Mexica precinct, was replaced by the current one in a project intended to symbolize the power of the Church in the Viceroyalty. The cathedral occupies more than 5,000 m^2 and features five naves, fourteen side chapels, two bell towers, and a sacristy of great artistic richness. Its interior highlights include the Altar de los Reyes, the choir with its carved stalls, and works by artists such as Juan Correa, Cristóbal de Villalpando, and Manuel Tolsá, who was responsible for the Neoclassical design of the main facade, the tabernacle, the high altar, and the dome. Throughout its history, it has faced earthquakes, fires, and differential sinking of the terrain. In the 1990s, it underwent a extensive restoration due to damage accumulated from seismic activity and the instability of the lacustrine subsoil. From its atrium, one can appreciate the viceregal layout of the Centro Histórico and, attached to the right side, the Sagrario Metropolitano, whose Baroque portal in *Chiluca* and *tezontle* stone constitutes one of the greatest examples of Novohispanic architecture.

Did you know...?
During its restoration in the 1990s, a permanent system for monitoring ground subsidence was implemented using sensors and millimeter-precision leveling, making the cathedral an international reference in structural conservation.

34

Monumento hipsográfico Estatua de Enrico Martínez

Address
C. de Monte de Piedad 7,
Col. Centro
Metro
Zócalo / Tenochtitlan Station,
Line 2
Metrobús
República de Chile Station and
República de Argentina Station,
Line 4
Ecobici
CE-089

Next to the Cathedral stands a monument commemorating Enrico Martínez, the royal cosmographer who led the drainage project for the Cuenca de México, one of the most ambitious and controversial endeavors of the viceregal period. In the early seventeenth century, following a series of floods in the Novohispanic capital, Martínez proposed opening artificial canals to drain the lakes surrounding the city, an intervention that transformed the region's lacustrine environment.

Although his proposal prevented some floods, he was criticized for calculation errors and for contributing to the progressive drying of the lakes that defined the Valley of Mexico. The hypsographic monument preserves one of the historical water levels as a testimony to a technical decision that modified the ecological and urban destiny of the city.

35

Plaza e Iglesia de Santo Domingo

Address
Belisario Domínguez s/n,
Col. Centro
Metro
Allende Station, Line 2
Garibaldi y Lagunilla Station,
Lines 8 and B
Metrobús
Glorieta Violeta Station,
Line 7
Ecobici
CE-091

Did you know...?
The Iglesia de Santo Domingo was the tallest building in Mexico City between 1754 and 1813, until it was surpassed by the Catedral Metropolitana.

This square represents one of the most outstanding examples of the permanence of the viceregal legacy in the city. Configured in the sixteenth century as part of the former Dominican convent, it was for centuries a meeting point between the religious, administrative, and commercial life of the viceregal capital. Upon entering from República de Brasil Street, an esplanade opens up, framed by historical constructions, where the Iglesia de Santo Domingo stands out as an example of eighteenth-century Solomonic Baroque, featuring twisted columns and reliefs of saints. Facing the temple is the Antiguo Palacio de la Santa Inquisición, the current seat of the Museo de la Medicina Mexicana, with its Neoclassical facade; and to one side, the Antigua Aduana de México, whose *tezontle* walls harken back to viceregal commerce. The perimeter arrangement of these buildings, together with the Portal de los Evangelistas, forms an urban ensemble of notable historical coherence. Touring Santo Domingo allows one to recognize the transition between Tenochtitlan and the viceregal city, a process visible in the open layout and the continuity of its urban uses.

36

Museo del Templo Mayor

Address
Seminario 8, Col. Centro
Metro
Zócalo / Tenochtitlan Station, Line 2
Metrobús
República de Argentina Station, Line 4
Ecobici
CE-094
Hours
Tue-Sun 9:00 - 17:00 h
Entry
Paid admission (includes archaeological zone and Museo del Templo Mayor), free on Sundays

Just behind the Catedral Metropolitana lie the vestiges of the most important building of the Mexica capital: the Templo Mayor. This precinct was the religious, political, and symbolic core of Tenochtitlan and functioned as the city's *axis mundi*. It was dedicated simultaneously to Huitzilopochtli, the god of war, and Tláloc, the god of the rain, expressing the balance between military power and agricultural fertility. Each expansion marked the reign of a new *tlatoani* and was built over the previous one, which is why at least seven superimposed construction stages have been identified. According to chronicles, the temple reached nearly 45 m in height and was visible from any point on the island. From its summit, priests performed human sacrifices that guaranteed the continuity of the cosmos. In front of the staircase lay the monolith of Coyolxauhqui, associated with the myth of the birth of Huitzilopochtli. Following the fall of Tenochtitlan in 1521, the conquistadors destroyed the temple and erected buildings of the viceregal period upon its ruins. Today, the Museo del Templo Mayor allows visitors to tour the original ruins and observe pieces such as the recently discovered Tlaltecuhtli, the biggest Mexica sculpture found to date.

Did you know...?
The Museo del Templo Mayor, open to the public in 1987, was designed by Pedro Ramírez Vásquez and conceived in accordance with what the Templo Mayor meant to the Tenochcas: the northern half is dedicated to Tláloc, god of the rain, and the southern half to Huitzilopochtli, god of war.

37

Mercado de la Lagunilla

Address
República de Ecuador 59J,
Col. Centro
Metro
Garibaldi y Lagunilla Station,
Lines 8 and B
Lagunilla Station, Line B
Metrobús
Garibaldi Station, Line 7
República de Chile Station,
Line 4

Did you know...?
The Sunday *tianguis* of La Lagunilla brings together collectors, curious onlookers, and design lovers seeking objects from nineteenth-century Mexico, such as tube radios, posters, cameras, and folk art.

El Mercado de la Lagunilla is one of the oldest commercial spaces in the city. Its origins date back to the viceregal period, when the area served as a key point of exchange on the northern edge of the urban grid. Since then, it has remained a continuous site of trade and circulation of objects, linked to practical knowledge of buying and selling as well as the preservation of material goods. Its most distinctive feature is the sale of antiques, especially pieces from the nineteenth century. Every weekend, the market turns into a specialized open-air bazaar offering furniture, clocks, tableware, lamps, prints, and decorative objects from old houses in the historic center and traditional neighborhoods. These pieces evoke nineteenth-century Mexico, the Porfiriato, and the local adoption of European styles, as well as transformations in domestic life and forms of social representation.

38

Centro Cultural Universitario Tlatelolco (CCUT)

Address
Av. Ricardo Flores Magón 1, Col. Nonoalco Tlatelolco
Metro
Tlatelolco Station, Line 3
Metrobús
Manuel González Station, Line 1
Hours
Wed-Thu 11:00 - 17:00 h
Fri-Sun 11:00 - 18:00 h
Entry
Paid admission

Did you know...?
For several years, the building served as the headquarters of the Secretaría de Relaciones Exteriores.

The CCUT, located at an emblematic point in Mexico City, is a space where history, memory, and culture converge. Its presence recalls the symbolic value of a territory where pre-Hispanic echoes intertwine with the viceregal and modern traces of the capital. Inaugurated in 2001, the complex gathers spaces dedicated to reflection and art. The CCUT offers a comprehensive reading of the past, from Mexica life to contemporary urban transformation. The center also includes a library, an auditorium, and exhibition halls. Its architecture, conceived by Pedro Ramírez Vázquez, stands out for its integration of the past and present. Linked to the Plaza de las Tres Culturas, the cultural center also evokes Indigenous resistance and the events of the Student Movement of 1968. The CCUT consolidates itself as a space where history and creation dialogue to keep collective memory alive.

39

Plaza de las Tres Culturas

Address
Eje Central Lázaro Cárdenas s/n, Col. Nonoalco Tlatelolco
Metro
Tlatelolco Station, Line 3
Metrobús
Glorieta Cuitláhuac Station, Line 7

Did you know...?
This site reveals how Mexico City is a palimpsest of cultures, as described by Guillermo Tovar de Teresa.

The Plaza de las Tres Culturas is a place of profound historical symbolism. Three fundamental moments of national history converge in this square: pre-Hispanic, viceregal, and modern Mexico. The vestiges of the ancient Mexica city of Tlatelolco, the sixteenth-century Iglesia de Santiago, and contemporary buildings form an ensemble where time overlaps in visible layers. The site was the setting for the most important market of the pre-Hispanic world and, centuries later, the events of October 2, 1968. On that day, a multitude of students demanding freedom and democracy was violently repressed, leaving a deep wound in the collective memory. Today, the Plaza de las Tres Culturas remains a space for reflection and homage. Amidst ruins, stone, and concrete, the place recalls the greatness of the original civilizations and the resistance of those who, in different times, have fought for a more just and free Mexico.

40

Iglesia y Antiguo Convento de Santiago Tlatelolco

Address
Plaza de las Tres Culturas s/n, Col. Nonoalco Tlatelolco
Metro
Tlatelolco Station, Line 3
Metrobús
Glorieta Cuitláhuac Station, Line 7
Hours
Mon-Sun 9:00 - 17:00 h

Did you know...?
The blue and red stained-glass windows, inspired by the local stone used in the church, were designed by Mathias Goeritz (1964), along with the golden altarpiece and the Stations of the Cross.

Located atop the remains of the ancient ceremonial center of Mexico-Tlatelolco, this Franciscan complex was built in the sixteenth century as part of the evangelization process following the fall of the Mexica.
The Iglesia de Santiago, begun around 1535 with stone from pre-Hispanic temples, follows the fortress-church model characteristic of early Franciscan constructions. Its gray quarry stone facade and the Baroque tower added in the seventeenth century preserve the memory of the place where the final battle of the conquest occurred on August 13, 1521. The use of repurposed materials evidences the superimposition of traditions and the integration of the Mexica past into the new viceregal architecture. To one side lies the Antiguo Convento and the Colegio de la Santa Cruz, considered the first institution of higher education in America intended for Indigenous youth. A notable intellectual exchange took place in this space, marking the cultural life of the region. The complex remained for centuries as a center for study, evangelization, and cultural transmission, and today it forms an essential part of the historical landscape of Tlatelolco.

41

Museo de Tecpan

Address
Reforma Norte 630, Col. Nonoalco Tlatelolco
Metro
Tlatelolco Station, Line 3
Metrobús
Tres Culturas Station, Line 7
Hours
Mon-Sun 9:00 - 17:00 h
Entry
Free admission

Did you know...?
In the mural, Siqueiros depicts Cuauhtémoc wielding weapons in opposition to the destruction of his civilization by the Spanish conquistadors.

This building was constructed immediately after the conquest of Mexico-Tenochtitlan to function as the government house and seat of the City Council of Santiago Tlatelolco, charged with governing the republic of Indians of the same name. The seven-span arcade of its ground floor dates from the sixteenth century and appears in the Codex Tlatelolco of 1563. During the Porfiriato, the columns of the upper floor were attached when the property was used as an orphanage. The main facade, built in the eighteenth century, was dismantled in 1962 and moved to the rear of the Colegio de la Santa Cruz de Tlatelolco during the construction of the urban complex Conjunto Habitacional Nonoalco Tlatelolco. The building houses the mural *Cuauhtémoc contra el mito*, created by David Alfaro Siqueiros in 1944. It is the author's first mixed-media plastic work, in which he combines modern paints with wood and Masonite supports, as well as sculptures created by Luis Arenal Bastar. Through a three-dimensional perspective, Siqueiros seeks to recreate the movement of the figures.

42

Zona Arqueológica de Tlatelolco

Address
Eje Central Lázaro Cárdenas s/n, Col. Nonoalco Tlatelolco
Metro
Tlatelolco Station, Line 3
Metrobús
Glorieta Cuitláhuac Station, Line 7
Hours
Mon-Sun 08:00 - 17:00 h
Entry
Paid admission

Did you know...?
The ancient market described by Bernal Díaz del Castillo as clean, orderly, and abundant was discovered in the Tlatelolco area.

Tlatelolco was founded around 1337, on the shores of Lake Texcoco, north of Tenochtitlan. Recognized for its role as a great commercial center, it housed the vastest and busiest market in the pre-Hispanic world, where cacao, feathers, textiles, tools, and food from all over Mesoamerica were exchanged. It was also the scene of political tensions with its neighbor Tenochtitlan, with whom, despite tensions, it shared the Nahuatl language and the same political system. Bernal Díaz del Castillo, in his *Historia verdadera de la conquista de la Nueva España*, describes the magnitude of that market, where up to 60,000 people were counted daily. However, the prosperity of Tlatelolco was affected by floods and political tensions with its neighbor. In 1521, following the latter's fall, Tlatelolco became the last bastion of Mexica resistance. Today, its archaeological zone preserves the memory of a city that was a symbol of commerce, power, and perseverance.

43

Conjunto Habitacional Nonoalco Tlatelolco

Address
Col. Nonoalco Tlatelolco
Metro
Tlatelolco Station, Line 3
Metrobús
Glorieta Cuitláhuac Station and Tres Culturas Station, Line 7
Ecobici
CE-540

Did you know...?
The design of Tlatelolco was based on principles of European modern urbanism: buildings raised on pilotis, shared open spaces, and separation between pedestrian and vehicular circulation, following Le Corbusier's functional model.

Designed by architect Mario Pani in the 1960s, this urban complex represents one of the most ambitious bets of Mexican modernism. Conceived as a city within the city, the project integrated more than 100 apartment buildings, schools, gardens, shopping centers, and a modern church within a rational and functionalist design. Inspired by the ideas of Le Corbusier and his "Radiant City," Pani sought to order urban chaos and offer dignified and modern housing for thousands of people through a high-density vertical model. It was built on the grounds of the ancient Indigenous neighborhood of Tlatelolco, integrating the Mexica archaeological zone, the sixteenth-century Temple of Santiago, and the new concrete towers into what Pani himself called "the trilogy of the three cultures": indigenous, viceregal, and modern. Over time, the project faced structural problems and gradual abandonment. The 1985 earthquake marked a decisive moment with the tragedy of the Nuevo León building. As a consequence of these earthquakes, a total of eight buildings had to be demolished and another four reduced in height. In the place where the Nuevo León building stood, a sundial can be seen today, where a line marks the time the earthquake occurred on September 19, 1985.

44

Museo Indígena, Antigua Aduana de Peralvillo

Address
Paseo de la Reforma Norte 707, Col. Morelos
Metro
Tlatelolco Station, Line 3
Metrobús
Peralvillo Station, Line 7
Hours
Mon-Sun 11:00 - 17:00 h
Entry
Free admission

Did you know...?
As the city's northern boundary, taxes were assessed here on all goods entering Mexico City.

At the end of the eighteenth century, the building that today houses the Museo Indígena was built; it functioned for decades as a *garita* (guard station) for collecting taxes on pulque, the most appreciated drink of viceregal Mexico. Due to its history and architectural value, it was declared a national monument in 1931. Currently, the Museo Indígena, Antigua Aduana de Peralvillo, belonging to the Instituto Nacional de los Pueblos Indígenas, is a space dedicated to dialogue and the valuation of Mexico's cultural diversity.

Its collection includes pieces dating from 1605 to the present: textiles, ceramics, lacquerware, feather art, metals, toys, musical instruments, and ritual objects from various Indigenous and Afro-Mexican peoples. The museum promotes the preservation and dissemination of cultural heritage through exhibitions, workshops, musical presentations, dances, and gastronomic showcases. In this precinct, the presence and participation of original communities are essential, consolidating a living space where memory and contemporary creation coexist in balance.

45

Calzada de los Misterios

Location
Between Acueducto de Guadalupe and Glorieta de Peralvillo
Metro
Villa-Basílica Station, Line 6
Misterios Station, Line 5

Did you know...?
The fifteen altars that today mark the Calzada de los Misterios were built in the seventeenth century and represent the Joyful, Sorrowful, and Glorious Mysteries of the Holy Rosary along the ancient Camino de Tepeyacac.

The Camino a Tepeyac, today Calzada de los Misterios, is an ancient Nahuatl trace north of Mexico City. Together, with the Camino de Tenayuca, it constitutes one of the works constructed by Tepanec and Mexica engineers. The technology used allowed these roads to function as processional routes and dikes to control flooding in the riparian zone of Lake Texcoco. This double function was present since pre-Hispanic times, as it allowed transit through the area while protecting the settlements established in its surroundings. *Tepeyac* or *Tepeyacac*, which means "the nose" in Nahuatl, was a peninsula where a population linked to a cave dedicated to Coatlicue-Tonantzin was established before the Spanish arrival. Throughout time, the Camino de Tepeyac–Calzada de los Misterios maintained its relationship with the region's religious practices, preserving its processional character. Since the seventeenth century, the causeway has included fifteen altars related to the Mysteries of the Holy Rosary, distributed between the Glorieta de Peralvillo and the Basílica de Guadalupe.

46

Basílica de Guadalupe

Address
Fray Juan de Zumárraga 2,
Col. Villa Gustavo A. Madero

Metro
La Villa-Basílica Station, Line 6
Deportivo 18 de Marzo Station, Line 3

Metrobús
La Villa Station, Line 6

Hours
Mon-Sun 6:00 - 21:00 h

Entry
Free admission

On the hill of Tepeyac, north of Mexico City, stands the Basílica de Guadalupe, one of the most visited sanctuaries in the world. Before the Conquest, Tepeyac was a sacred site dedicated to Tonantzin, a mother deity linked to fertility. With evangelization, the place acquired new meaning following the apparitions of 1531 to Juan Diego, as the Virgin's image remained imprinted on his *tilma* (cloak). Devotion grew, and successive temples were built until the basilica was inaugurated in 1976, designed by Pedro Ramírez Vázquez. Its circular form allows thousands of pilgrims to contemplate the original *tilma* up close, a symbol of faith and union between Indigenous and Spanish cultures. Next to the complex stand the Capilla del Pocito and the Museo Mariano, with liturgical and artistic pieces linked to the Guadalupan cult. This event was interpreted as a symbol of the evangelization, as the Virgin of Guadalupe began to be seen as a figure who united the indigenous people and the Spanish. Juan Diego's *tilma* is the most important object of religious veneration in Mexico, visited and celebrated every December 12.

Did you know...?
The ancient seventeenth-century basilica began to sink starting in the late nineteenth century due to the lacustrine subsoil. For decades, the building remained visibly tilted, and masses were officiated with an uneven altar. To prevent its collapse, the new basilica was built in 1976 with a modern structure and deep foundations, designed to adapt to the unstable terrain of the north of the city.

3

Between the white marble of the Palacio de Bellas Artes and the music that fills Plaza Garibaldi there is one of Mexico City's most significant corridors. This route brings together different moments in the history of the capital, linking spaces that reflect the evolution of its architecture, public life, and artistic expressions.

Bellas Artes / Garibaldi

The starting point is the Palacio de Bellas Artes, open to the public in 1934 after a lengthy construction process interrupted by the Revolution and various structural adjustments. Its architecture combines *art nouveau* and *art déco* elements, a synthesis that reflects the country's modernizing aspirations during the first third of the twentieth century. Inside are some of the most representative murals of modern Mexican art. The building replaced former viceregal theaters, including the now-lost Coliseo de Comedias and Teatro Nacional, consolidating a cultural space that symbolizes the institutionalization of art in post-revolutionary Mexico.

Beside the palace lies the Alameda Central, the oldest park in America. It was laid out in 1592 by order of Viceroy Luis de Velasco as a tree-lined promenade for the New Spanish elite. Across the centuries, it has undergone numerous urban interventions that altered its layout, urban furniture, and vegetation. In the eighteenth century, the Mariscala Fountain marked the arrival of water from the viceregal aqueduct from Chapultepec, recalling the role of the hydraulic system in the Basin of Mexico. Today, the park maintains its original function as a place of gathering and rest, integrating past and present within the urban landscape.

Facing the Alameda, the Museo Franz Mayer, housed in the former San Juan de Dios convent, holds one of the most important collections of decorative arts in Latin America. Its holdings of silverwork, ceramics, textiles, and furniture offer insight into daily life and cultural exchanges during the viceregal era and the nineteenth century. A few blocks away, the Kaluz Museum, located in an eighteenth-century Baroque hospice, presents a contemporary vision of Mexican art through a collection that links pictorial traditions with current perspectives.

Another emblem of the city stands out along this route: the Monument to the Revolution. Originally conceived as the seat of a grand parliamentary building, it was transformed into a site of historical reflection by one of the key architects for understanding Mexico City in the first half of the twentieth century, Carlos Obregón Santacilia.

The historic Buenavista station reflects the profound impact that the railroad had on nineteenth-century Mexican society and today serves as a crucial hub of urban transportation.

The route concludes in Garibaldi, an emblematic center of Mexican popular music and nightlife. This urban axis, which connects cultural institutions, public spaces, and popular expressions, encapsulates the continuities and manifestations that characterize Mexico City.

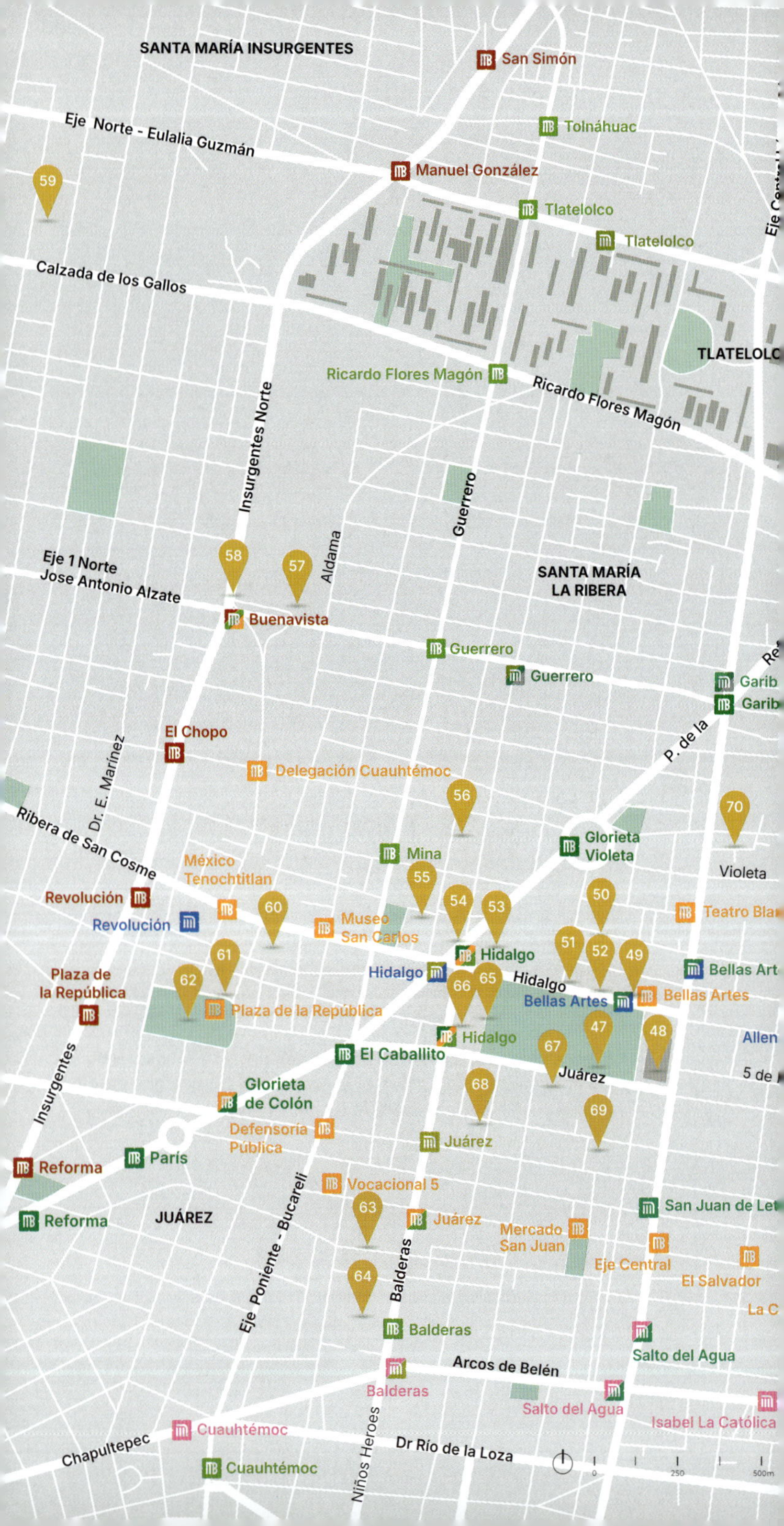
SANTA MARÍA INSURGENTES
San Simón
Tolnáhuac
Eje Norte - Eulalia Guzmán
Manuel González
59
Tlatelolco
Tlatelolco
Calzada de los Gallos
TLATELOLCO
Ricardo Flores Magón
Ricardo Flores Magón
Insurgentes Norte
Guerrero
Aldama
Eje 1 Norte
Jose Antonio Alzate
58
57
SANTA MARÍA
LA RIBERA
Buenavista
Guerrero
Guerrero
Garib
Garib
P. de la
El Chopo
Delegación Cuauhtémoc
Dr. E. Marínez
56
70
Ribera de San Cosme
Glorieta
Violeta
Mina
Violeta
México
Tenochtitlan
55
Revolución
60
54
53
50
Teatro Bla
Revolución
Museo
San Carlos
Hidalgo
51
52
49
61
Bellas Art
Plaza de
la República
62
Hidalgo
66
65
Hidalgo
Bellas Artes
Bellas Artes
Plaza de la República
47
48
Hidalgo
Allen
El Caballito
67
Juárez
5 de
Glorieta
de Colón
68
Insurgentes
69
Defensoría
Pública
Juárez
Reforma
París
Vocacional 5
San Juan de Let
Reforma
JUÁREZ
63
Juárez
Mercado
San Juan
Eje Poniente - Bucareli
Eje Central
El Salvador
64
Balderas
La C
Balderas
Salto del Agua
Arcos de Belén
Balderas
Salto del Agua
Isabel La Católica
Cuauhtémoc
Chapultepec
Niños Heroes
Dr Río de la Loza
Cuauhtémoc
0
250
500m

Route 3 / Bellas Artes-Garibaldi

47 Alameda Central

48 Palacio de Bellas Artes

49 Museo Nacional de la Estampa (MUNAE)

50 La Nana

51 Plaza de la Santa Veracruz

52 Museo Franz Mayer

53 Museo Kaluz

54 Templo de San Hipólito

55 Museo Panteón de San Fernando

56 Casa Rivas Mercado

57 Biblioteca Vasconcelos

58 Antigua Estación de Ferrocarriles de Buenavista

59 Fundación Casa Wabi – Sabino

60 Museo Nacional de San Carlos

61 Frontón México

62 Monumento y Museo Nacional de la Revolución

63 Mercado de Artesanías de La Ciudadela

64 Biblioteca de México

65 Laboratorio Arte Alameda

66 Museo Mural Diego Rivera

67 Museo Memoria y Tolerancia

68 Museo de Arte Popular (MAP)

69 Barrio Chino

70 Plaza Garibaldi

47

Alameda Central

Address
Av. Hidalgo s/n, Col. Centro
Metro
Bellas Artes Station, Lines 2 and 8
Hidalgo Station, Lines 2 and 3
Metrobús
Hidalgo Station, Lines 3, 4, and 7
Ecobici
CE-043, CE-052

The Alameda Central is the oldest public park in America. Founded in 1592 by order of Viceroy Luis de Velasco, its purpose was to beautify an unpopulated area on the outskirts of the viceregal city. Its name comes from the poplars (*álamos*) planted at that time, and from the beginning, it was conceived as an orderly promenade for rest and social gathering. Over time, it ceased to be peripheral to become integrated into the urban heart of Mexico City, transforming into a place of meeting and social representation. During the eighteenth and nineteenth centuries, multiple interventions were carried out: fountains, benches, sculptures, lampposts, and geometric paths were added. At one time it was completely fenced, a symbol of social control over public spaces, and during the Porfiriato it was consolidated as an open promenade, decorated with monuments to historical figures such as Beethoven, Benito Juárez, and Ignacio Ramírez "El Nigromante." Diego Rivera portrayed it in *Sueño de una tarde dominical en la Alameda Central*, a mural that brings together more than four centuries of national history.
The 1985 earthquake marked a turning point in its urban environment following the collapse of neighboring buildings. Today, surrounded by the Palacio de Bellas Artes, the Museo Franz Mayer, and the Torre Latinoamericana, the Alameda continues as an open, wooded space and a witness to the daily life of the center.

Did you know...?
In Mexico City, jacarandas fulfill a symbolic role similar to cherry trees in Japan. Though they seem native, they were introduced in the twentieth century and now signal the arrival of spring across the city's urban landscape.

48

Palacio de Bellas Artes

Did you know...?
It has been the most emblematic venue for posthumous tributes to artists such as Silvia Pinal, Juan Gabriel, José José, and Frida Kahlo. During Kahlo's ceremony, that the coffin was covered with the Communist Party flag, which created an uncomfortable moment for the authorities of the time.

Address
Av. Juárez s/n, Col. Centro
Metro
Bellas Artes Station, Lines 2 and 8
Metrobús
Bellas Artes Station, Line 4
Ecobici
CE-052, CE-043
Hours
Tue-Sun 10:00 - 18:00 h
Entry
Paid admission, free on Sundays

To one side of the Alameda Central rises one of the most emblematic venues of Mexican cultural life, the result of a construction process that began in 1904 under the direction of Italian architect Adamo Boari. The original project, with modernist lines and neoclassical references, faced ground subsidence, the Mexican Revolution, and technical limitations that prolonged the work for decades. These delays defined a building where twentieth-century modern engineering, European tradition, and an aesthetic identity inspired by Mexico's artistic expressions coexist.

The exterior, entirely clad in Carrara marble, is complemented by a facade featuring sculptures by Leonardo Bistolfi and mythological motifs. The dome, finished in ochre and golden tones, changes slightly depending on light conditions throughout the day. Inside, the lobby utilizes Mexican marble and polished metals under a functionalist logic that privileges spatial clarity. Its walls shelter an exceptional set of murals by Diego Rivera, David Alfaro Siqueiros, José Clemente Orozco, Rufino Tamayo, Rina Lazo, and Roberto Montenegro, conceived as a space for dialogue between architecture and artistic practice. The main hall, intended for opera, dance, and symphonic concerts, incorporates precisely studied acoustics and a Tiffany glass curtain depicting the Popocatépetl and Iztaccíhuatl volcanoes. The venue houses museums, archives, and spaces dedicated to artistic research and dissemination, as well as the seasons of the Compañía Nacional de Ópera, the Compañía Nacional de Danza, and the Orquesta Sinfónica Nacional. Its permanent activity sustains it as a benchmark of rigor, elegance, and cultural continuity.

49

Museo Nacional de la Estampa (MUNAE)

Did you know...?
The MUNAE collection includes works by José Guadalupe Posada, creator of *La Catrina*, and artists such as Ilya Kabakov and Richard Serra.

Address
Av. Hidalgo 39,
Col. Guerrero
Metro
Hidalgo Station, Line 2 and 3
Bellas Artes Station, Lines 2 and 8
Metrobús
Hidalgo Station, Line 3
Bellas Artes Station, Line 4
Ecobici
CE-052
Hours
Tue-Sun 10:00 - 18:00 h
Entry
Paid admission, free on Sundays

Located in a nineteenth-century neoclassical building in Plaza de la Santa Veracruz, the Museo Nacional de la Estampa, or MUNAE, is the main venue dedicated to graphic arts in Mexico. Inaugurated in 1986, it protects one of the most important collections in the country, with more than 12,000 pieces ranging from pre-Hispanic clay stamps to contemporary works. Its permanent exhibition traverses the main stages of engraving—pre-Hispanic, viceregal, academic, modern, and contemporary—distributed across three thematic halls. In addition to preserving graphic heritage, the museum promotes workshops, guided tours, and a printing laboratory, with an emphasis on technical experimentation and the teaching of graphic art. The building stands on the former grounds of the cemetery of the Santa Veracruz parish, demolished between 1833 and 1842. Its adaptation in 1986, by presidential decree, consolidated the recognition of engraving as a fundamental expression of Mexican cultural heritage.

50

La Nana

Address
2do Callejón San Juan de Dios 25, Col. Guerrero
Metro
Bellas Artes Station, Lines 2 and 8
Metrobús
Bellas Artes Station, Line 4
Ecobici
CE-052
Hours
Mon-Fri 9:00 - 19:00 h
Sat 9:00 - 13:00 h
Entry
Free admission

Did you know...?
In this space, each workshop cycle concludes with a presentation open to the public, where participants of different ages share their creative processes and become familiar with the stage as part of their artistic training.

Located in an early twentieth-century industrial heritage building formerly occupied by the Salón México, this urban laboratory of socially engaged art functions as the headquarters of the Consorcio Internacional Arte y Escuela A.C. Coordinated by ConArte, it is a meeting space where school and community converge through a program integrating workshops, exhibitions, and cultural activities open to all types of audiences. Its courses are designed for children, youth, and adults to approach disciplines such as dance —in contemporary, ballroom, folkloric, and urban styles— music, visual arts, plastic arts, handicrafts, and trades. With a quarterly duration, the sessions seek to adapt to the participants' daily lives and conclude with public showcases that strengthen the formative process, addressing current social issues and generating spaces for dialogue that drive neighborhood coexistence.

51

Plaza de la Santa Veracruz

Address
Av. Hidalgo 45,
Col. Centro
Metro
Bellas Artes Station, Lines 2 and 8
Metrobús
Bellas Artes Station, Line 4
Ecobici
CE-052

Did you know...?
The plaza is slightly lower than Avenida Hidalgo. To access it, one descends a few steps, a vestige of land adjustments made over five centuries, a difference in level that gives it a particular character.

This space, located behind the Alameda Central, corresponds to the ancient atrium of the Iglesia de la Santa Veracruz and, due to its original layout, is one of the oldest squares in the city, with antecedents from the sixteenth century. The site is flanked by two historical temples: the Iglesia de la Santa Veracruz and the Iglesia de San Juan de Dios, formerly the chapel of the Hospital de los Desamparados and today linked to the nearby Museo Franz Mayer. This environment forms a heritage complex where viceregal architecture, past ceremonial practices, and the daily activity of the Centro Histórico coexist. Throughout the centuries, the plaza has had diverse uses. It was the site of popular markets, such as the Mercado de las Flores in the 1920s, and functioned as an open-air forum during the 1968 Olympic Games. Currently, with its trees, benches, and a central fountain, the plaza operates as a resting space integrated into the daily movement of the area.

52

Museo Franz Mayer

Address
Av. Hidalgo 45,
Col. Centro
Metro
Bellas Artes Station, Lines 2 and 8
Metrobús
Bellas Artes Station, Line 4
Ecobici
CE-052, CE-043
Hours
Tue-Sun 10:00 - 17:00 h
Entry
Paid admission, free on Sundays

Did you know...?
In his final years, Franz Mayer organized his collection with the idea that it would become a public museum. Far from elitist collecting, he recognized aesthetic value in the domestic and the functional.

Opposite from the Alameda Central, in the former Hospital de San Juan de Dios, lies the Museo Franz Mayer, inaugurated in 1986. It gathers the collection of German businessman Franz Mayer Traumann, who arrived in Mexico in the early twentieth century and dedicated his life to collecting European and New Spanish decorative art: furniture, textiles, ceramics, clocks, silverware, painting, and old books. The building, of sober viceregal architecture, preserves a central courtyard surrounded by quarry stone arches that functions as a natural prelude to the tour. The museography privileges detailed observation and appreciation of artistic craftsmanship. In addition to its permanent collection, the museum organizes exhibitions of design, photography, fashion, and folk art, and is the venue for the International Poster Biennial. It features a library specialized in art and design, one of the most complete in the country, as well as a cafeteria and shop.

53

Museo Kaluz

Did you know...?
The museum's exterior mural, *Jardín Urbano*, created by Vicente Rojo, is made with high-temperature ceramic mosaics reflecting the visual diversity of Mexican art without using explicit symbols.

Address
Av. Hidalgo 85,
Col. Guerrero
Metro
Hidalgo Station, Lines 2 and 3
Metrobús
Hidalgo Station, Lines 3, 4, and 7
Bellas Artes Station, Line 4
Ecobici
CE-052
Hours
Wed-Mon 10:00 - 18:00 h
Entry
Paid admission

The Museo Kaluz is located at the corner of Reforma and Avenida Hidalgo, in a historic building that functioned as a hospice since the eighteenth century. Safeguards a collection of Mexican, Japanese, and Spanish exile art spanning more than four centuries. Furthermore, the museum hosts temporary exhibitions, educational activities, and a sculpture garden on its terrace. The building where the museum is housed today is situated on what was the ancient aqueduct path connecting Santa Fe with Mexico City. This layout is precisely represented in the Trasmonte plan of 1628, where the water line is observed crossing the western zone toward the viceregal center. The property formed part of the urban framework that consolidated transit between the high valley and the lacustrine capital.

54

Templo de San Hipólito

Address
Francisco Zarco 12, Col. Centro
Metro
Hidalgo Station, Lines 2 and 3
Metrobús
Hidalgo Station, Lines 3, 4, and 7
Ecobici
CE-043
Hours
Mon-Sun 7:00 - 20:00 h

Did you know...?
The church towers are rotated forty-five degrees relative to the facade because they were built following the orientation of the ancient Mexico-Tacuba causeway, keeping the original viceregal layout of the land visible.

The Templo de San Hipólito y San Casiano was built over the hermitage ordered by Hernán Cortés after the so-called Noche Triste—the defeat suffered in the early hours of June 30, 1520—to honor the fallen Spaniards. Construction of the current building began in 1599 and concluded in 1740, consolidating a baroque temple that perpetuates that event within the ancient layout of the Mexico-Tacuba causeway, the main route by which the conquistadors fled. In 1559, an annex hospital was founded, considered the first dedicated to people with mental health issues on the American continent. Throughout its history, the complex also served as barracks and a school. In the twentieth century, it transformed into a center of devotion to Saint Jude Thaddeus, attracting thousands of pilgrims on the 28th of every month. Its atrium preserves commemorative monuments evoking the historical character of the site and its relevance in urban memory.

55

Museo Panteón de San Fernando

Address
C. San Fernando 17, Col. Centro
Metro
Hidalgo Station, Lines 2 and 3
Metrobús
Hidalgo Station, Lines 3, 4, and 7
Ecobici
CE-043
Hours
Tue-Sun 11:00 - 17:00 h
Entry
Free admission

Did you know...?
In niche number 19 appears the name of the dancer Isadora Duncan, who never visited Mexico. It is believed the plaque was placed as a tribute promoted by Plutarco Elías Calles, an admirer of her art.

The Museo Panteón de San Fernando is one of the most representative cemeteries of the nineteenth century in Mexico City and was established as a museum in 2006. Founded in 1832 next to the temple of San Fernando, it functioned until 1872 as a burial space for figures such as Benito Juárez. Its funerary architecture —tombs, niches, and sculptures— preserves the neoclassical aesthetic of the era, while information panels address liberalism and the ideals of the Reform. Originally, it was part of the atrium of the former Convent of San Fernando and was the first public pantheon outside of churches. In 1859, with Juárez's law on the secularization of cemeteries, it became the Pantheon of Illustrious Men. Closed after the burial of Juárez himself in 1872, it was declared a historical monument in 1936 and reopened as a museum in 2006. It offers guided tours, events, and night tours.

56

Casa Rivas Mercado

Address
C. Héroes 45, Col. Guerrero
Metro
Hidalgo Station, Lines 2 and 3
Metrobús
Mina Station, Line 3
Ecobici
CE-265, CE-268-269
Hours
Sat-Sun 10:00 - 12:00 h
Entry
Paid admission

Did you know...?
The upper floor houses the office where the most important work was carried out: the column of the Monumento de la Independencia.

In the heart of Colonia Guerrero stands the Casa Rivas Mercado, one of the most notable mansions of the Porfiriato. Designed by architect Antonio Rivas Mercado, its construction lasted from 1893 to 1897 as a personal project reflecting an eclectic and residential aesthetic vision.
The residence combined classical elements, such as Doric columns and Renaissance balustrades, Moorish motifs in friezes and tiles, *art nouveau* details, and a structure of American oak and quarry stone. The encaustic tiles were imported from England, with more than 50,000 pieces in dozens of designs. The house was inhabited by the Rivas Mercado family until the architect's death in 1927, and in 1936 it was donated to the Church; afterward, it functioned as a school and later as housing. After a long period of abandonment in the second half of the twentieth century, it was restored, and since 2017 serves as a cultural center and as a space dedicated to the architect.

57

Biblioteca Vasconcelos

Address
Eje 1 Norte s/n, Col. Buenavista
Metro
Buenavista Station, Line B
Metrobús
Buenavista Station, Lines 1, 3, and 4
Ecobici
CE-266, CE-267
Hours
Mon-Sun 8:30 - 19:30 h

Did you know...?
The botanical garden surrounding the library integrates more than 168 plant species and was designed as a living tribute to José Vasconcelos, in consonance with his vision of education as part of the country's cultural identity.

The Biblioteca Vasconcelos is one of the most relevant cultural infrastructures built in Mexico in the twenty-first century, resulting from an international competition. Inaugurated in 2006, this library was conceived as a large-scale educational project whose architectural design made it a contemporary landmark of the city due to its structural and material complexity and its incorporation of natural light and passive ventilation. Designed by architect Alberto Kalach together with Juan Palomar, Tonatiuh Martínez, and Gustavo Lipkau, it occupies 38,000 m^2 and combines steel, glass, and concrete in a structure where shelves seem to float on multiple suspended levels. The building is surrounded by a botanical garden conceived as a transition between the built environment and its urban surroundings, establishing a bridge between nature, culture, and learning. The venue bears the name of José Vasconcelos (1882-1959), philosopher, lawyer, and first Secretary of Public Education, and houses more than 600,000 volumes, reading rooms, a sound archive, children's areas, multimedia spaces, and a gallery. Prominent in its interior is the work *Mátrix Móvil* by plastic artist Gabriel Orozco, a gray whale bone structure.

58

Antigua Estación de Ferrocarriles de Buenavista

Address
Av. Insurgente Norte s/n, Col. Buenavista
Metro
Buenavista Station, Line B
Metrobús
Buenavista Station, Lines 1, 3, and 4
Ecobici
CE-266, CE-267

Did you know...?
The wagon that transported the body of Benito Juárez in 1872 departed from this station. Commemorative trains for the Centennial of Independence in 1910 and military convoys during the Mexican Revolution also departed from here.

Located north of the Centro Histórico, the Antigua Estación de Ferrocarriles de Buenavista was the neuralgic point of the central railway system of the country for more than a century. Officially inaugurated in 1873 during the government of Sebastián Lerdo de Tejada, it was the first major modern infrastructure project of independent Mexico. With the arrival of the railroad, Buenavista became the departure and arrival point for passenger and freight trains connecting the capital with major industrial, port, and agricultural centers. The station, in a sober neoclassical style, was expanded and modernized in later decades, consolidating itself as a symbol of national railway development. At the end of the twentieth century, competition from road transport and lack of investment caused a reduction in passenger service. The station closed in 1999 and was rehabilitated in 2008 as the terminal for the Tren Suburbano, preserving part of its original structure. Today its surroundings integrate the Forum Buenavista shopping center and the Biblioteca Vasconcelos.

59

Fundación Casa Wabi – Sabino

Did you know...?
The transformation of its headquarters, carried out with minimal intervention, preserves original structural elements that allow an understanding of the neighborhood's productive past.

Address
Sabino 336,
Col. Atlampa
Metro
San Cosme Station, Line 2
Buenavista Station, Lines 1 and B
Metrobús
Buenavista Station,
Lines 1, 3, and 4
Ecobici
CE-537
Hours
Tue-Sun 10:00 - 17:00 h
Entry
Free admission

This foundation dedicated to the exhibition and dissemination of contemporary art is part of a project with a presence in Oaxaca—where its artist residency is located—and in Tokyo. Its headquarters in Mexico City are located within a building adapted for galleries, terraces, and artistic production areas. Its connection to an international network of artistic creation makes this venue a relevant point on the city's cultural map. Its location in Atlampa responds to a commitment to cultural decentralization. Installed in an old industrial neighborhood, this venue promotes new creative practices in an area traditionally removed from the most visible artistic circuit. Inaugurated in 2023, this space aims to offer an accessible and flexible platform for emerging and established artists. Its programming includes periodic exhibitions and experimental projects. One of its distinctive features is its open policy for new proposals, supporting a diversity of languages and perspectives.

60

Museo Nacional de San Carlos

Address
Av. México-Tenochtitlan 50, Col. Tabacalera
Metro
Revolución Station, Line 2
Metrobús
Museo San Carlos Station, Line 4
Ecobici
CE-450
Hours
Tue-Sun 10:00 - 18:00 h
Entry
Paid admission, free on Sundays

Did you know...?
The museum preserves one of the three existing Gothic altarpieces in Mexico: the *Retablo de la Encarnación* from the fifteenth century, an exceptional piece due to its age, its Marian iconography, and its remarkable state of conservation.

The Museo Nacional de San Carlos houses a collection of European paintings, sculptures, and engravings ranging from the fourteenth to the early twentieth century. Located in the former Palacio del Conde de Buenavista, it was inaugurated in 1968 by the Instituto Nacional de Bellas Artes y Literatura (INBAL) and declared a National Museum in 1994. Its collection includes works by Rubens, Goya, Ingres, Sorolla, and masters linked to the ancient Academia de San Carlos, the axis of artistic education in New Spain. The permanent halls, organized by movements, allow visitors to traverse the evolution of Western painting. The palace was built between 1798 and 1805 by architect Manuel Tolsá for the Count of Buenavista. It is distinguished by its oval courtyard, unique in the city. During the nineteenth century, it was the residence of distinguished figures, such as Antonio López de Santa Anna, and in the twentieth century, it housed a cigar factory, offices of the Lotería Nacional, and a high school.

61

Frontón México

Address
Av. de la República 17,
Col. Tabacalera
Metro
Revolución Station, Line 2
Metrobús
Plaza de la República Station,
Lines 1 and 4
Ecobici
CE-270
Hours
Mon-Sun 10:00 - 17:00 h

Did you know...?
It hosted several world championships, as well as competitions for the 1968 Olympic Games.

Inaugurated on May 10, 1929, Frontón México was the first roofed venue in the country dedicated to the practice of Basque pelota. Its *art déco* architecture and its sporting and social vocation made it one of the symbols of modernity in the capital. Designed by architects Teodoro Kunhardt and Joaquín Capilla, the building is distinguished by its reinforced concrete structure, its quarry stone and marble facade, and its spacious column-free interiors. Located opposite the Monumento a la Revolución, it functioned actively as a center for spectacles, betting, and sports until 1996, when a union strike forced its closure. After two decades of abandonment, it was rehabilitated and reopened in 2017 as a multifunctional space combining sports, culture, and entertainment. Today it hosts *jai alai* matches, concerts, theater, exhibitions, and a casino, reaffirming its emblematic character in urban life.

62

Monumento y Museo Nacional de la Revolución

Address
Av. de la República s/n,
Col. Tabacalera
Metro
Revolución Station, Line 2
Metrobús
Plaza de la República Station,
Lines 1 and 4
Ecobici
CE-270
Hours
Mon-Thu 12:00 - 20:00 h
Fri-Sat 12:00 - 22:00 h
Sun 10:00 - 20:00 h
Entry
Paid admission, free on Sundays

Located in Plaza de la República, the Monumento a la Revolución is one of the most recognizable public spaces in Mexico City. Its copper dome, monumental columns, and mixture of architectural styles reflect the history of its construction and the symbolic meaning it holds. The project originated during the Porfiriato as the Federal Legislative Palace, designed by Émile Bénard in 1910, but was interrupted by the Revolution. In the 1930s, Carlos Obregón Santacilia transformed the unfinished structure into a commemorative monument. At its base rest the remains of Francisco I. Madero, Venustiano Carranza, Francisco Villa, Plutarco Elías Calles, and Lázaro Cárdenas. The museum occupying its subterranean levels, inaugurated in 1986, presents a visual, documentary, and symbolic reading of the revolutionary process and its repercussions throughout the twentieth century. The halls cover the Porfirian regime, the armed conflict, the Constitution of 1917, and post-revolutionary governments. In 2010 its museography was updated with interactive technological resources. The ascent to the observation deck, at a height of more than 60 m, allows observation of the metallic structure of the ancient palace and a panoramic view of the city center. The surrounding esplanade is today a civic and cultural space that continues to host public acts, fairs, and concerts.

Did you know...?
In 1933, a call was issued for the creation of the sculptures for the Monumento a la Revolución. Oliverio Martínez was selected as a finalist with his project *Transformation*, a group of 11-meter-high sculptures. *Independence*, *Labor Laws*, *Reform Laws*, and *Agrarian Laws* were installed on each of the monument's pillars.

63

Mercado de Artesanías de La Ciudadela

Address
Balderas s/n,
Col. Centro
Metro
Juárez Station,
Line 3
Metrobús
Vocacional 5 Station,
Line 4,
Juárez Station,
Lines 3 and 4
Ecobici
CE-098
Hours
Mon-Sat 10:00 - 19:00 h
Sun 10:00 - 18:00 h

Did you know...?
The original name of the venue is Mercado Artesanal Mexicano, but it is known as "La Ciudadela" due to the neighborhood where it is located. Some tenants have kept their family stall for more than three generations.

At the southern limit of the Centro Histórico lies one of the most representative markets for Mexican folk art. Inaugurated in 1965 as part of the cultural program for the 1968 Olympic Games, this space was conceived to gather the country's most outstanding artisans in a single place. Since then, it has functioned as a meeting point between cultures, traditions, and national and international visitors. Walking through its aisles, one observes *alebrijes* from Oaxaca, textiles from Chiapas and Guerrero, ceramics from Michoacán, wooden toys, musical instruments, amate paper, saddlery, and palm work. Each piece reflects traditional techniques transmitted from generation to generation. Unlike temporary markets or *tianguis*, La Ciudadela offers stable conditions for more than 300 tenants from the 32 states of the country, with fixed stalls in wood and tile structures. Its proximity to Balderas Station and the Biblioteca de México makes it an ideal stop to discover the diversity of folk art.

64

Biblioteca de México

Address
Plaza de La Ciudadela 4,
Col. Centro
Metro
Balderas Station,
Lines 1 and 3
Metrobús
Balderas Station,
Line 3
Ecobici
CE-098, CE-107-108
Hours
Mon-Sun 8:30 - 19:30 h

Did you know...?
This ancient Tobacco Factory had spacious courtyards for drying and transporting raw material. The courtyards, adapted without losing their original layout, today allow for the open distribution of halls and reading areas.

Located in La Ciudadela building—built at the end of the eighteenth century as the Royal Tobacco Factory of New Spain— this venue has had diverse functions throughout its history: barracks, political prison, military warehouse, and hospital. Its solid structure, with thick walls and interior courtyards, retains the industrial character with which it was conceived. The transformation of the property into a public library began in the 1940s, driven by José Vasconcelos, who proposed gathering a national collection open to the public. Inaugurated in 1946, the institution began with nearly 40,000 volumes coming from private collections and ancient academic libraries. In 1987, a deep remodeling directed by Abraham Zabludovsky reorganized the interior spaces. Subsequently, in 2011, the project "La Ciudadela–City of Books" renovated halls, incorporated specialized areas, digital spaces, a children's area, an exhibition hall, and personal collections of various intellectuals.

65

Laboratorio Arte Alameda

Did you know...?
The Centro de Documentación Príamo Lozada preserves more than 20,000 audiovisual records, photographs, and montages, making it one of the most complete archives of electronic art in Mexico.

Address
Dr. Mora 7,
Col. Centro
Metro
Hidalgo Station, Lines 2 and 3
Metrobús
Hidalgo Station, Line 3
Bellas Artes Station, Line 4
Ecobici
CE-043
Hours
Tue-Sun 9:00 - 17:00 h
Entry
Paid admission, free on Sundays

Located in the former Convent of San Diego, opposite the Alameda Central, the Laboratorio Arte Alameda is a space dedicated to the creation, research, and exhibition of projects linking art and technology. The original building dates from 1591 and across from it stood the burning site of the Holy Inquisition. After the Reform Laws, it had various uses until becoming, in 1964, the Pinacoteca Virreinal. It was re-inaugurated in 2000, redefining its vocation and presenting video installations, interactive works, net art, and multimedia shows conceived to dialogue with its historical architecture—chapel, cloisters, and main nave—which forms an essential part of the artistic proposals. This space promotes workshops, seminars, concerts, and experimental film cycles. It features the Centro de Documentación Príamo Lozada, which safeguards archives, videos, and technical records, consolidating itself as a benchmark in digital and electronic art.

66

Museo Mural Diego Rivera

Address
Colón s/n,
Col. Centro
Metro
Hidalgo Station, Lines 2 and 3
Metrobús
Hidalgo Station, Line 3
Bellas Artes Station, Line 4
Ecobici
CE-043
Hours
Tue-Sun 10:00-18:00 h
Entry
Paid admission, free on Sundays

Did you know...?
In the mural, Diego Rivera represents himself as a child with a toad inside his pocket, a reference to his nickname, el Sapo.

The Museo Mural Diego Rivera is dedicated to the fresco *Sueño de una tarde dominical en la Alameda Central*, created by Diego Rivera between July and September 1947. The work, measuring 5 × 16 m, brings together more than 150 figures representing the history of Mexico from the Conquest to the Revolution. Among them stand out La Catrina, José Guadalupe Posada, Frida Kahlo, and Rivera himself portrayed in his childhood. The museum was built to preserve the mural after the 1985 earthquake, which destroyed the Hotel del Prado, its original venue. The piece was moved using a specially designed metal structure, and the venue was inaugurated in 1988, incorporating temporary exhibitions and activities on muralism. Commissioned by Carlos Obregón Santacilia for the dining room of the Hotel del Prado, the fresco evoked life in the Alameda Central and the historical memory of the country.

67

Museo Memoria y Tolerancia

Did you know...?
The suspended cube of the building symbolizes the fragility of human coexistence, a visual reminder of the balance necessary for peace and tolerance.

Address
Av. Juárez 8, Col. Centro
Metro
Hidalgo Station, Lines 2 and 3
Juárez Station, Line 3
Metrobús
Hidalgo Station, Lines 3, 4, and 7
Bellas Artes Station, Line 4
Ecobici
CE-043
Hours
Tue-Fri 9:00 - 18:00 h
Sat-Sun 10:00 - 19:00 h
Entry
Paid admission, free on Sundays

Located opposite the Alameda Central, the Museo Memoria y Tolerancia is one of the most significant and urgent spaces in Mexico City. Inaugurated in 2010, it was conceived as a place of conscience to remember the horrors caused by intolerance and to promote a culture of respect for human rights. The tour is divided into two sections: memory and tolerance. In the first, some of the darkest episodes of the twentieth century are documented, such as the Holocaust and the genocides in Armenia, Rwanda, Cambodia, and Bosnia, through original objects, testimonies, and immersive settings that confront the visitor with human brutality. In the second part, topics such as racism, homophobia, inequality, and hate speech are addressed from a reflective and pedagogical perspective, inviting active and critical reflection. Designed by Arditti + RDT Arquitectos, the building combines sobriety and symbolism. Its clean-lined structure and controlled use of light create an introspective environment that accompanies the sense of the tour.

68

Museo de Arte Popular (MAP)

Did you know...?
The MAP houses a "Tree of Life" more than 4 m high, a work by Alfonso Soteno from Metepec, and a hall dedicated to *lucha libre* as a popular cultural expression of the twentieth century.

Address
Revillagigedo 11, Col. Centro
Metro
Juárez Station, Line 3
Metrobús
Hidalgo Station, Lines 3, 4, and 7
Ecobici
CE-048
Hours
Tue-Sun 10:00 - 18:00 h
Entry
Paid admission, free on Sundays

Inaugurated in 2006, the MAP is the country's most important institutional space dedicated exclusively to Mexican folk art. It is located in the former building of the General Police and Firefighters Inspection, a 1928 property with an *art déco* facade covered in tiles and neocolonial elements, restored and adapted for museum functions at the beginning of the twenty-first century. The MAP safeguards a collection representing the diversity of Mexico's artisanal traditions. Its permanent halls are organized by materials and techniques, allowing observation of links between objects from different regions: textiles, papier-mâché (*cartonería*), ceramics, wood, blown glass, masks, miniatures, *alebrijes*, toys, lacquerware, and vegetable fibers. The museum proposes a critical and heritage-based reading of folk art, addressing themes such as religious syncretism, transmission of knowledge, innovation, and daily life. Each year it organizes the Noche de los Alebrijes, a public parade with monumental figures created by artisanal collectives.

69

Barrio Chino

Address
Av. Independencia 32,
Col. Centro
Metro
San Juan de Letrán Station,
Line 8
Metrobús
Eje Central Station, Line 4
Ecobici
CE-082

Did you know...?
It is a landmark destination for Asian cuisine in the city. There is also a traditional pharmacy where medicinal teas and products imported from Asia are still sold.

Unlike the Chinatowns of other capitals, this is not a large colony nor an ethnically homogeneous community, but a symbolic zone preserving the memory of the first Chinese migrations to Mexico, which occurred between 1880 and 1940. At the end of the nineteenth century, merchants and workers originally from Canton (Guangdong) began to settle in this central area. Many worked as laundrymen, cooks, or shopkeepers, and over time they opened cafes, pharmacies, and restaurants. During the revolutionary period and until the mid-twentieth century, the community faced episodes of discrimination and violence, such as the killing of Chinese people in Torreón in 1911. The current Barrio Chino was delimited in the 1990s as a cultural and tourist initiative by the local government and entrepreneurs of Chinese origin. Arches, lanterns, plaques with Chinese characters, and thematic street furniture were installed. Today it functions as a commercial and gastronomic corridor, especially busy during the celebration of the Chinese New Year.

70

Plaza Garibaldi

Address
Eje Central Lázaro Cárdenas 43, Col. Centro
Metro
Garibaldi y Lagunilla Station, Lines 8 and B
Metrobús
Garibaldi Station, Line 7
Ecobici
CE-091

Did you know...?
The plaza bears the name of Giuseppe Garibaldi, a nineteenth-century Italian hero, in recognition of his defense of the republican and liberal causes that inspired several political movements in Latin America.

Famous for being the heart of Mexican music, especially mariachi, Plaza Garibaldi was inaugurated in 1851 and has since been a meeting point between tradition and popular life. Its history is linked to the cultural transformation of Mexican music, with mariachi groups beginning to perform in its surroundings at the end of the nineteenth century. The place has been the stage for national manifestations and celebrations, as well as multiple representations of the urban imaginary. Over time, it has been renovated to offer a contemporary experience, with restaurants, bars, and terraces. Although active throughout the day, it comes alive at night, when musicians gather to play for visitors.
The plaza has also hosted other genres of Mexican popular music, reinforcing its diverse and symbolic character.

4

Chapultepec

Chapultepec, whose name in Náhuatl means "hill of the grasshopper," has been one of the most strategic, symbolic, and contested spaces in the Basin of Mexico since pre-Hispanic times. Its history begins long before the founding of Tenochtitlan. Various peoples of the high plateau, among them the Tepanecs and later the Mexica, identified this wooded hill as a primary source of fresh water, a defensive enclave, and a place with religious significance.

In the late thirteenth or early fourteenth century, Mexica groups who had not yet settled permanently began to establish themselves in the Chapultepec area. From there, they attempted to form an autonomous community until they were expelled by the Tepanecs of Azcapotzalco, whose power dominated the western side of the lake. This defeat led to a period of wandering until, under the protection of the same Tepanecs, the Mexica settled on the lake's islets and founded Tenochtitlan around 1325. Despite this early exile, Chapultepec remained part of the Mexica symbolic horizon as a place of ritual and ecological importance.

With the arrival of the Spaniards, Chapultepec was recognized for its strategic value. Hernán Cortés granted these lands to the Crown, and the viceregal government later turned the area into a place for rest and hunting. In the sixteenth century, a small chapel was built, and in the eighteenth century Viceroy Bernardo de Gálvez ordered the construction of a summer residence on the hill. That structure, transformed and expanded, became the origin of the present-day Chapultepec Castle.

Beginning in 1822, after independence, the building was used by various governments. In 1841 it was officially designated as the seat of the Military College, marking its symbolic transition into a space of patriotic education and national defense. During the U.S. invasion of 1847, the castle was the site of the Battle of Chapultepec.

During the Porfiriato, the forest was developed as a public recreational space inspired by European models of urban parks. Avenues were laid out, new tree species were planted, and sculptures and fountains were added. Throughout the twentieth century, Chapultepec was formally incorporated into the national park system and divided into sections. Museums, zoos, auditoriums, and sports areas were built within it. Its history reflects the transformation of the territory from the sacred to the public, from the defensive to the civic.

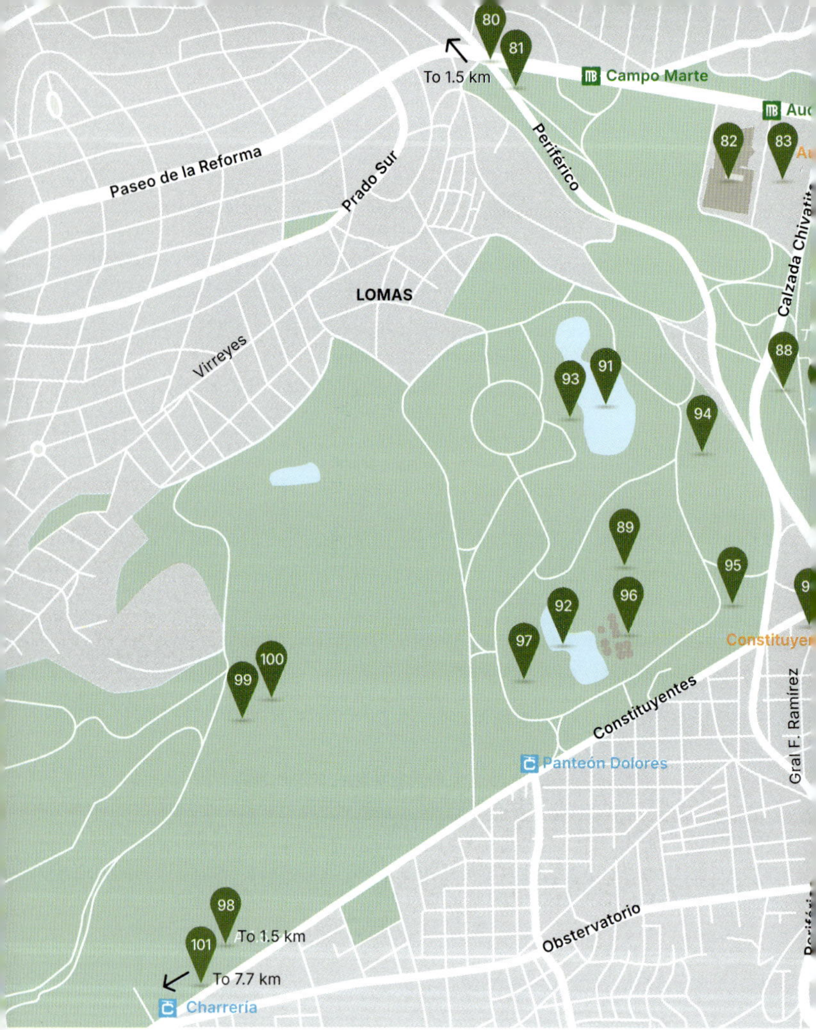

Route 4 / Chapultepec

71 Centro de Cultura Digital (CCD) / Estela de Luz

72 Museo de Arte Moderno (MAM)

73 Museo Nacional de Historia Castillo de Chapultepec

74 Museo del Caracol / Galería de Histori

75 Baños de Moctezuma

76 Jardín Botánico de Chapultepec

77 Zoológico de Chapultepec

78 Museo Tamayo

79 Museo Nacional de Antropología

80 Museo Jumex

81 Museo Soumaya

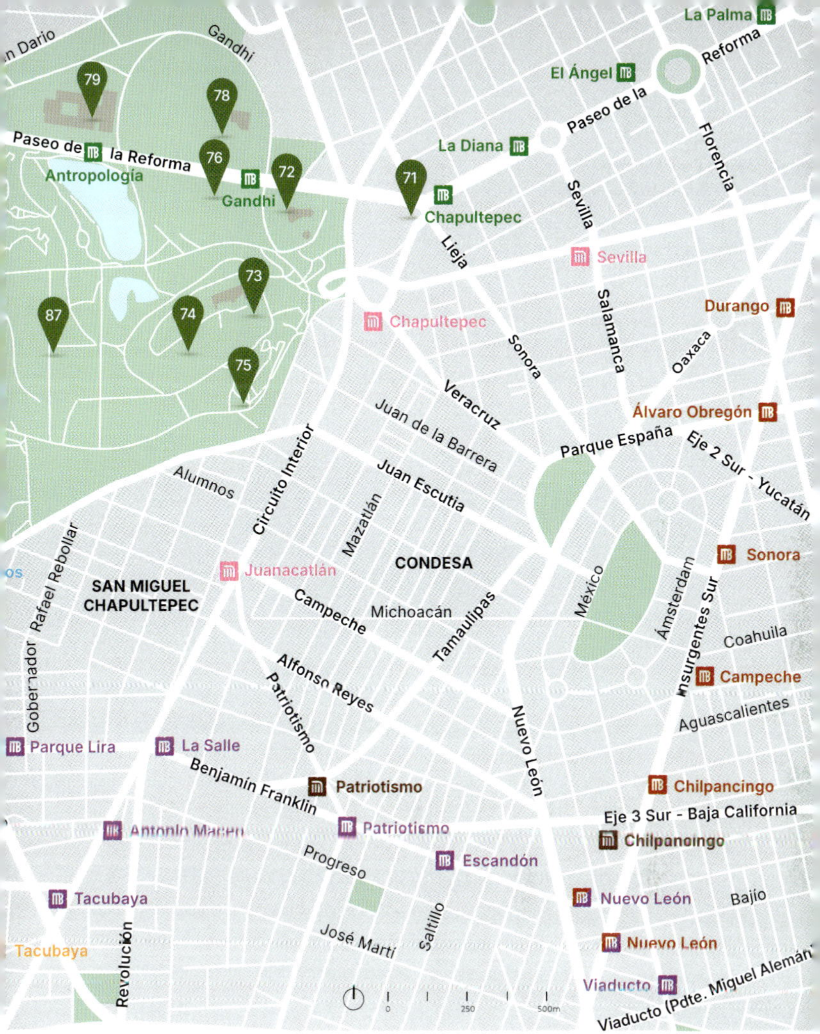

82 Auditorio Nacional

83 Jardín Escénico

84 Monumental Fuente de Nezahualcóyotl

85 Complejo Cultural Los Pinos

86 Cencalli: Casa del Maíz y la Cultura Alimentaria

87 Fuente del Quijote

88 Calzada Flotante

89 Museo del Cárcamo de Dolores y Fuente de Tláloc

90 Casa Ortega / Casa Estudio Luis Barragán

91 Lago Mayor

92 Lago Menor

93 Lago Algo

94 Aztlán Parque Urbano (Aztlán Feria de Chapultepec)

95 Papalote Museo del Niño

96 Parque Ecológico / Centro de Cultura Ambiental (CCA)

97 Museo de Historial Natural y Cultura Ambiental

98 Parque de Cultura Urbana (PARCUR)

99 Serpiente y escaleras

100 Panteón Civil Dolores

101 Cineteca Nacional Chapultepec

102 Cablebús Chapultepec

71

Centro de Cultura Digital (CCD) / Estela de Luz

Address
Paseo de la Reforma s/n, corner with Lieja, Col. Juárez
Metro
Chapultepec Station, Line 1
Metrobús
Chapultepec Station, Line 7
Ecobici
CE-007, CE-014
Hours
Tue-Sun 11:00 - 18:00 h
Entry
Free admission

Did you know...?
The CCD was the first public space in Mexico designed specifically to exhibit and produce digital art, and its "Memorial" room is a pioneer in interactive light installations.

The Estela de Luz, one of the most visible contemporary monuments on Paseo de la Reforma—the original endpoint of the avenue in its nineteenth-century plan— houses at its base a key project for understanding technological creation in Mexico City: the Centro de Cultura Digital (CCD). The Estela de Luz, 104 m high, is formed by steel columns covered with quartz plates that capture natural light. Beneath this vertical volume lies the CCD, which reuses the monument's underground space as a platform for laboratories, halls, and forums dedicated to digital culture. It features areas for exhibition, cinema, a forum for performing arts, workshops, and a multimedia room specialized in sound and interactive art. The relationship between the monumentality of the Estela and the subtlety of the CCD creates a dialogue between commemorative memory and contemporary creation.

72

Museo de Arte Moderno (MAM)

Did you know...?
The painting *Las dos Fridas* by Frida Kahlo is part of the museum's collection and is usually exhibited as one of its most emblematic central pieces.

Address
Av. Paseo de la Reforma s/n, Col. Bosque de Chapultepec I Sección
Metro
Chapultepec Station, Line 1
Metrobús
Gandhi Station, Line 7
Ecobici
CE-194
Hours
Tue-Sun 10:15 - 17:45 h
Entry
Paid admission, free on Sundays

The MAM is one of the main institutions dedicated to twentieth-century art in Mexico. Its collection and temporary exhibitions allow for a critical overview of the country's modern and contemporary visual arts. Inaugurated in 1964 as part of a cultural program, the museum consolidated itself as a space for the conservation, study, and dissemination of national artistic production. Conceived in the context of the great cultural projects of the 1960s, the MAM was developed in parallel to the Museo Nacional de Antropología. Architects Pedro Ramírez Vázquez and Rafael Mijares Alcérreca designed a set of circular pavilions immersed in the Bosque de Chapultepec, integrating halls, lobbies, and a sculpture garden. Since its origin, the museum assumed pedagogical and heritage functions, with a collection comprising works by Rufino Tamayo, Remedios Varo, Leonora Carrington, David Alfaro Siqueiros, and José Clemente Orozco, among others. Today its collection exceeds 3,000 pieces, organized in nuclei addressing aesthetic modernity, abstraction, surrealism, the Rupture, and other currents of the Mexican twentieth century.

73

Museo Nacional de Historia Castillo de Chapultepec

Did you know...?
Chapultepec Castle is the only castle in the Americas. Beneath its foundations, pre-Hispanic remains have been found.

Address
Col. Bosque de Chapultepec
I Sección
Metro
Chapultepec Station, Line 1
Metrobús
Gandhi Station and Chapultepec Station, Line 7
Ecobici
CE-194
Hours
Tue-Sun 9:00 - 17:00 h
Entry
Paid admission, free on Sundays

Built on the summit of the Chapulín Hill, the Castillo de Chapultepec constitutes one of the most significant historical complexes in the country. Its history summarizes three centuries of political, social, and territorial transformations. Conceived in 1785 by order of Viceroy Bernardo de Gálvez as a rest house, the castle remained unfinished after his death and was resumed with different purposes over time.
In 1841 it was assigned to the Military College, where the Battle of Chapultepec took place on September 13, 1847, during the American invasion. With the Second Mexican Empire, it was restored as the residence of Maximilian of Habsburg and Charlotte, who adapted its architecture and gardens according to European tastes. Later, various presidents inhabited it until Lázaro Cárdenas converted it into the headquarters of the Museo Nacional de Historia in 1939. The ascent to the castle begins at the Puerta de los Leones, flanked by two bronze sculptures, it functions as a symbolic threshold between Paseo de la Reforma and the forest, announcing the ascent toward the hill and its historical memory.

74

Museo del Caracol / Galería de Historia

Did you know...?
In the museum, there is a hall dedicated to the Constitution of 1917. Conceived as a secular chapel, Chávez Morado sculpted a quarry stone eagle that presides over the enclosure.

Address
Col. Bosque de Chapultepec I Sección
Metro
Chapultepec Station, Line 1
Metrobús
Gandhi Station and Chapultepec Station, Line 7
Ecobici
CE-194
Hours
Tue-Sun 9:00 - 16:15 h
Entry
Paid admission, free on Sundays

The Museo del Caracol, officially called Galería de Historia, is a unique museographic venue in Mexico. Inaugurated on November 21, 1960, by President Adolfo López Mateos, it was conceived as part of the commemorations of the Sesquicentennial of Independence and the Centennial of the Revolution, with the purpose of offering the public—especially students—a clear and chronological vision of national history from 1810 to 1917. Designed by architect Pedro Ramírez Vázquez, the building is located on the ramp leading to Castillo de Chapultepec and stands out for its helicoidal structure, which gives it its popular name, *el Caracol* (The Snail). Throughout several levels, the visitor traverses a sequence constructed through models, dioramas, reliefs, sculptures, and maps that present, in a didactic way, episodes such as the Grito de Dolores, the entry of the Trigarante Army, the Reform War, the French Intervention, the Porfiriato, the Mexican Revolution, and the promulgation of the 1917 Constitution. Although it responds to twentieth-century civic nationalism, the museum remains valid as a pedagogical tool; its curatorial script has been updated to incorporate new historiographical readings.

75

Baños de Moctezuma

Address
Av. Heroico Colegio Militar s/n, Col. Bosque de Chapultepec I Sección
Metro
Chapultepec Station, Line 1
Ecobici
CE-258
Hours
Mon-Sun 8:00 - 18:00 h

Did you know...?
Chapultepec was a sacred ritual and ecological space for the Mexicas. Ceremonies of power renewal were performed here. The aqueduct built to transport water from these springs reached the center of Tenochtitlan.

The so-called Baños de Moctezuma are one of the few pre-Hispanic hydraulic vestiges preserved *in situ* in the Bosque de Chapultepec. They are located on the northern slope of the hill, between the Lago Mayor and the Museo de Sitio, protected by a fence and marked as an archaeological monument. Despite their name, they were not recreational baths, but part of a ceremonial and functional hydraulic system that supplied water to Mexico-Tenochtitlan. Their origin dates back to the fifteenth century, during the governments of Moctezuma Ilhuicamina and Moctezuma Xocoyotzin, who ordered the channeling of the Chapultepec springs through aqueducts and distribution boxes. The complex is formed by a rectangular pool, stairways, stone walls, and a stepped structure that allowed regulating the flow of water toward the aqueduct crossing the Tlacopan causeway (today Mexico-Tacuba). After the conquest, the system continued in use during the viceroyalty but was abandoned with the desiccation of the basin. Rediscovered in the nineteenth century, the site was protected in the twentieth century and remains under the care of the INAH.

76

Jardín Botánico de Chapultepec

Address
Av. Paseo de la Reforma 126, Col. Bosque de Chapultepec I Sección
Metro
Chapultepec Station, Line 1
Metrobús
Gandhi Station, Line 7
Ecobici
CE-195
Hours
Tue-Sun 9:00 - 16:00 h

Did you know...?
The garden houses a collection of young *ahuehuetes* descended from the historic trees of Chapultepec, as well as a sample of native maize from different regions of the country.

The Jardín Botánico de Chapultepec is one of the most important spaces dedicated to environmental education and flora conservation in Mexico City. Inaugurated in 2006 as part of the forest's comprehensive rehabilitation program, it occupies just over five hectares and houses more than 300 plant species, mainly Mexican. Its layout combines open areas and shaded paths organized into thematic collections: succulents and cacti, aquatic plants, medicinal plants, ornamental plants, and species endemic to the Basin of Mexico.

The garden fulfills a double function: it offers a space for recreation and, at the same time, seeks to raise awareness about the importance of native flora in an increasingly fragmented urban environment. It is distinguished by a monumental greenhouse with species from tropical and subtropical zones, as well as an orchidarium, a bamboo pavilion, and areas for workshops and exhibitions. Access is free, and the tour allows visitors to appreciate plant diversity in continuity with Chapultepec's historical vocation as a forest reserve.

77

Zoológico de Chapultepec

Address
Calzada Chivatito s/n,
Col. Bosque de Chapultepec
I Sección
Metro
Auditorio Station, Line 7
Metrobús
Auditorio Station, Line 7
Ecobici
CE-192, CE-193
Hours
Tue-Sun 9:00 - 16:30 h
Entry
Free admission

Did you know...?
The Zoológico de Chapultepec became renowned for its giant pandas. Xin Xin, its last resident, is the only panda outside China and the last in Latin America.

The Zoológico de Chapultepec is one of the oldest and most emblematic wildlife venues in Mexico City. Located in the first section of the Bosque de Chapultepec, it is part of a set of recreational, educational, and environmental facilities articulating this public space. Inaugurated in 1924, the zoo initially responded to a model of exotic fauna exhibition, which over time transformed into a vision centered on conservation and environmental education. Throughout the twentieth century, the venue renovated its facilities to improve animal welfare and update its museographic criteria. Currently, it participates in reproduction and protection programs for emblematic species, including at-risk native fauna such as the axolotl and the Mexican wolf, as well as species from other regions of the world. Through tours, signage, and outreach activities, the Zoológico de Chapultepec seeks to sensitize the public to biodiversity loss and the importance of ecosystems.

78

Museo Tamayo

Address
Av. Paseo de la Reforma 51, Col. Polanco I Sección
Metro
Auditorio Station, Line 7
Metrobús
Antropología Station, Line 7
Ecobici
CE-194, CE-195
Hours
Tue-Sun 10:00 - 18:00 h
Entry
Paid admission, free on Sundays

Did you know...?
Rufino Tamayo supervised the architecture and curation of the museum and requested spacious halls, without interior columns and with controlled light to preserve the experience of each work.

The Museo Tamayo is one of the most relevant spaces dedicated to contemporary art and reflection on artistic modernity from an international perspective. Founded in 1981 at the initiative of Oaxacan painter Rufino Tamayo, it was conceived as a platform for dialogue between Mexican art and global currents, integrating a critical vision of twentieth and twenty-first-century discourses into its architecture, collection, and programming. The project was consolidated in the 1970s thanks to the collaboration between the artist, the federal government, and the private sector. The building, designed by Teodoro González de León and Abraham Zabludovsky, is distinguished by exposed concrete, stepped volumes, and its integration into the Bosque de Chapultepec. The initial collection comes from Tamayo's personal collection and includes works by Joan Miró, Pablo Picasso, Mark Rothko, Francis Bacon, Roberto Matta, Alexander Calder, and the artist himself. Through its curatorial program, the museum has presented exhibitions of key figures in contemporary art, such as Louise Bourgeois, Hélio Oiticica, Tania Bruguera, James Turrell, and Gabriel Orozco, reinforcing its character as an international reference.

79

Museo Nacional de Antropología

Did you know...?
During its transfer from Texcoco where it was found in 1964, the monolith of Tláloc provoked a torrential rain, interpreted as a sign of its "awakening."

Address
Av. Paseo de la Reforma s/n, Col. Polanco I Sección
Metro
Auditorio Station, Line 7
Metrobús
Antropología Station, Line 7
Ecobici
CE-195
Hours
Tue-Sun 9:00 - 18:00 h
Entry
Paid admission, free on Sundays

Inaugurated on September 17, 1964, the Museo Nacional de Antropología is the most important archaeological and ethnographic venue in Mexico. Situated in the Bosque de Chapultepec, it symbolizes the Mexican State's effort to preserve, study, and disseminate the historical and cultural diversity of the territory. Its architecture, designed by Pedro Ramírez Vázquez, Jorge Campuzano, and Rafael Mijares Alcérreca, became an icon of mid-twentieth-century institutional modernity from its opening. The project, promoted during the government of Adolfo López Mateos, responded to the need to create a comprehensive space gathering the archaeological expressions of ancient Mexico and the cultural richness of contemporary indigenous peoples. The building was built in record time on land near the ancient Casa del Lago. Its central courtyard, covered by a large umbrella supported by a single column, has transformed into one of the most recognizable images of the Mexican cultural landscape. The permanent halls are organized into two great axes: archaeology and ethnography, with emblematic pieces such as the Piedra del Sol, the monolith of Tláloc, and numerous ritual and daily objects narrating the complex history of Mesoamerican civilizations.

80

Museo Jumex

Address
Miguel de Cervantes Saavedra 303, Col. Granada
Metro
San Joaquín Station and Polanco Station, Line 7
Ecobici
CE-197, CE-240, CE-462
Hours
Tue-Fri 10:00 - 17:00 h
Sat 10:00 - 19:00 h
Sun 10:00 - 17:00 h
Entry
Free admission

Did you know...?
Museo Jumex safeguards works from the Jumex Collection, one of the most significant private contemporary art collections in Latin America, with pieces by artists such as Cy Twombly, Gabriel Orozco, Jeff Koons, Donald Judd, and Andy Warhol.

Museo Jumex is an institution dedicated to contemporary art, inaugurated in 2013 as the main exhibition space of the Fundación Jumex Arte Contemporáneo. Since its inception, the foundation has been conceived as a project aimed at fostering the production, reflection, and dissemination of contemporary art at both national and international levels through exhibitions, publications, and public programs. Its curatorial approach combines the presentation of established artists with projects by emerging creators, as well as collaborations with curators and institutions from different parts of the world. The building—British architect David Chipperfield's first in Latin America—is defined by a sober volumetry and the use of nationally sourced materials, conceived to engage in dialogue with the urban context of Plaza Carso. The structure is organized over five levels—basement, ground floor, and three upper levels—which house exhibition galleries, service areas, and gathering spaces, with particular attention to the control of natural light.

81

Museo Soumaya

Did you know...?
The Museo Soumaya designed by Fernando Romero (FR-EE) is part of a network of cultural sites belonging to the Carlos Slim Foundation, located in different areas of Mexico City.

Address
Miguel de Cervantes Saavedra y Presa Falcón, Col. Granada
Metro
San Joaquín Station and Polanco Station, Line 7
Ecobici
CE-197, CE-240, CE 462
Hours
L-D 10:30 - 18:30 h
Entry
Free admission

The Museo Soumaya is an institution dedicated to the conservation, study, and dissemination of art collections spanning more than thirty centuries of art history. Founded by the Carlos Slim Foundation, it is distinguished by its public vocation and by a collection with broad chronological and geographical scope. The collection includes one of the most important concentrations of European art in Latin America, with works by the so-called Old Masters, among them Sandro Botticelli, El Greco, Tintoretto, and Peter Paul Rubens. Of particular note is the sculptural ensemble by Auguste Rodin—the most important outside France—presented in dialogue with works by Camille Claudel. The collection also features paintings from Impressionism and the historical avant-garde, as well as works by artists such as Giorgio de Chirico, Raoul Dufy, and Salvador Dalí. Art produced in Mexico occupies a central place in the curatorial discourse. The visit includes Mesoamerican pieces, paintings from the viceregal period and independent Mexico, and expressions from after the Mexican Revolution, with works by Diego Rivera, José Clemente Orozco, David Alfaro Siqueiros, and Rufino Tamayo.

82

Auditorio Nacional

Address
Col. Bosque de Chapultepec
I Sección
Metro
Auditorio Station, Line 7
Metrobús
Antropología Station, Line 7
Ecobici
CE-195
Hours
Box office Tue-Sun 9:00 - 16:30 h

Did you know...?
In 2007 a monumental organ with more than 15,000 pipes was installed; Juan Gabriel performed more than 200 concerts here during his lifetime.

The Auditorio Nacional, located on Paseo de la Reforma opposite the Bosque de Chapultepec, is one of the most important performing arts venues in the world and Mexico's main entertainment forum. With a capacity for around 10,000 people, it has hosted concerts, opera, dance, theater, cinema, official ceremonies, and international festivals. Inaugurated in 1952 as Auditorio de la Ciudad de México, it was intended for civic acts and equestrian activities in the context of the Pan American Games.
The original building, designed by Fernando Parra Hernández and Pedro Ramírez Vázquez, responded to a functionalist and monumental language. The new stage, concluded in 1991 by Teodoro González de León and Abraham Zabludovsky, transformed it into a world-class scenic box, with improved acoustics and sightlines and a brutalist image in black quarry stone. The spacious lobby, the Sala de Arte, the Lunario, and the esplanade with the Monument to Cantinflas and the United Nations fountain reinforce its character as a modern cultural symbol.

Justo
sky
TEMPUR

83

Jardín Escénico

Address
Av. Paseo de la Reforma 111,
Col. Bosque de Chapultepec
I Sección
Metro
Auditorio Station, Line 7
Metrobús
Auditorio Station, Line 7
Ecobici
CE-192-193, CE-237-238
Hours
Mon-Sun 8:00 - 20:00 h

Did you know...?
The Jardín Escénico was built on former vehicular grounds of the third section: its environmental recovery allowed the reforestation of more than four hectares with native and pollinator plants.

The Jardín Escénico is one of the most innovative cultural projects in the Bosque de Chapultepec. Conceived by the INBAL following a diagnosis of the needs of the performing arts at the Centro Cultural del Bosque, it seeks to reintegrate artistic creation with the natural environment. Designed by architect Isaac Michan, it occupies seven hectares organized under a principle of sustainability: only three buildings are inserted into a landscape restored with native species and pollinator areas. The central space is the Pabellón Escénico, whose structure allows the windows to be completely opened so performances can be enjoyed from the gardens, slopes, and paths. A few steps away, the Laboratorio de Creación Escénica promotes experimentation, professional training, and interdisciplinary collaboration, consolidating the complex as a true creative ecosystem.
The project also incorporates a wetland that captures rainwater and improves the environmental health of the area, and it will connect with the Chivatito Floating Causeway to articulate new cultural routes within the forest.

84

Monumental Fuente de Nezahualcóyotl

Address
Av. Heroico Colegio Militar, Col. Bosque de Chapultepec I Sección
Metro
Auditorio Station, Line 7
Metrobús
Auditorio Station, Line 7
Ecobici
CE-192, CE-193
Hours
Tue-Sun 6:00 - 18:00 h

Did you know...?
On the pedestal is inscribed a Nahuatl poem attributed to Nezahualcóyotl, and the fountain is symbolically oriented toward ancient Texcoco.

In the first section of the Bosque de Chapultepec, facing the Lago Mayor, stands the Fuente de Nezahualcóyotl, one of the most relevant monumental works of public art of the twentieth century in Mexico. Inaugurated in 1956, it was part of official programs for urban beautification and the recovery of pre-Hispanic memory. It was designed by sculptor Luis Ortiz Monasterio, who combined monumental sculpture and references to Mexica art to pay homage to Nezahualcóyotl (1402–1472), *tlatoani* of Texcoco, poet, legislator, and hydraulic builder. The complex is organized into a large semicircular exedra with a central sculpture 11 m high, carved in volcanic stone, representing the ruler in a contemplative attitude. To the sides, bas-reliefs display hydraulic symbols, glyphs, and scenes alluding to his engineering works. Also conceived as a monument to water, the fountain dialogues with the lacustrine landscape of the Lago Mayor and the access to the museum zone and the Botanical Garden.

85

Complejo Cultural Los Pinos

Address
Calzada del Rey s/n,
Col. Bosque de Chapultepec
I Sección
Metro
Constituyentes Station, Line 7
Cablebús
Los Pinos / Constituyentes Station, Line 3
Ecobici
CE-711
Hours
Tue-Sun 10:00 - 18:00 h

Did you know...?
The Casa Miguel Alemán preserves an underground bunker and a private cinema room, now open to the public as part of the tour.

The Complejo Cultural Los Pinos is a symbolic public space open since 2018. For more than eight decades it functioned as the official residence of the presidents of Mexico, from Lázaro Cárdenas to Enrique Peña Nieto. Its opening to the public implied a transformation in the use of this venue, which went from being a reserved sphere of executive power to a cultural complex with free access.
The origin of the complex dates back to the ancient Rancho La Hormiga, acquired by the Mexican State in the early twentieth century. In 1934, Lázaro Cárdenas decided not to inhabit Castillo de Chapultepec and moved the presidential residence to this property, which he renamed Los Pinos. In 2018, Andrés Manuel López Obrador opted not to use it as a residence and designated it for cultural activities. Currently, it hosts concerts, exhibitions, screenings, book presentations, and community gatherings, in addition to preserving furniture and rooms that allow visitors to observe how different leaders lived and governed.

86

Cencalli: Casa del Maíz y la Cultura Alimentaria

Address
Av. Parque Lira s/n,
Col. Bosque de Chapultepec
I Sección
Metro
Constituyentes Station, Line 7
Metrobús
Parque Lira Station, Line 2
Cablebús
Los Pinos / Constituyentes Station, Line 3
Ecobici
CE-711
Hours
Tue-Sun 11:00 - 18:00 h

Did you know...?
Cencalli protects one of the most complete public collections of native maize varieties in Mexico, gathered with the support of producers and seed custodians from all over the country.

Cencalli, the "Casa del Maíz y la Cultura Alimentaria," is one of the most significant projects of the Complejo Cultural Los Pinos. Installed in the historic Molino del Rey—an eighteenth-century building linked to the ancient Santa Fe aqueduct—this space was restored to reactivate its social vocation and serve as a museum dedicated to food, biodiversity, and community knowledge. Its proposal links architectural heritage, political memory, and peasant traditions. The project, part of Chapultepec: Naturaleza y Cultura, claims the centrality of maize in Mexican history through thematic halls, workshops, documentaries, and participatory spaces. Here, processes such as domestication, nixtamalization, and the *milpa* are explored, understood not only as agricultural techniques but as living cultural systems. The venue houses an agroecological market promoting encounters between traditional cooks, producers, and researchers.

87

Fuente del Quijote

Address
Calzada de los Filósofos s/n, Col. Bosque de Chapultepec I Sección
Metro
Juanacatlán, Line 1
Metrobús
Antropología Station, Line 7
Cablebús
Los Pinos / Constituyentes Station, Line 3
Ecobici
CE-195

Did you know...?
The Talavera decorating the fountain was produced by Puebla workshops in the 1920s, and several original pieces were able to be reintegrated during the recent restoration.

The Fuente del Quijote is one of the most symbolic spaces in the Bosque de Chapultepec, where literature, architecture, and nature integrate into an environment of contemplation. Built in 1921 on an octagonal platform surrounded by centuries-old *ahuehuete trees*, it was conceived as a tribute to *Don Quixote of La Mancha*, with four benches decorated with Talavera tiles illustrating key scenes from the novel. To the sides, two structures clad in the same material support bronze sculptures of Don Quixote and Sancho Panza, creating a small narrative stage around the water. In 1974 a sculpture of mermaids was incorporated into the upper basin, adding an ornamental accent to the ensemble. Recent restoration —part of the Chapultepec: Naturaleza y Cultura project— recovered Talavera tiles, floors, and landscaping, and removed the perimeter fence to fully reintegrate the fountain into pedestrian traffic. Today it is a place destined for reading, rest, and enjoyment of the forest's historical landscape.

88

Calzada Flotante

Address
Molino del Rey s/n,
Col. Bosque de Chapultepec
I Sección
Metro
Auditorio Station and
Constituyentes Station, Line 7
Metrobús
Auditorio Station, Line 7
Cablebús
Los Pinos / Constituyentes Station,
Line 3
Ecobici
CE-192, CE-193

Did you know...?
The Calzada Flotante forms part of the master project designed by Gabriel Orozco for Chapultepec; its layout protects centuries-old trees, guided by digital root studies.

The Calzada Flotante of Chapultepec is one of the most significant pedestrian infrastructure projects in recent public space in Mexico City. Conceived as an elevated corridor connecting the first and second sections of the Chapultepec forest, its design privileges visual lightness and full integration with the landscape. The structure is supported by discreet pillars and a thin steel and concrete platform that generates the sensation of moving "above" the terrain without altering the environment. The route offers open views toward the trees and the historic slopes of the hill, reinforcing the idea of a contemplative promenade. The low railing and sober geometry allow attention to focus on the continuity of the forest. More than a simple bridge, the causeway resolves an ancient disconnection between sections of the park through a functional, accessible, and respectful solution for natural heritage. Its soft lighting and clean layout have made it a benchmark of contemporary design in Mexico.

89

Museo del Cárcamo de Dolores y Fuente de Tláloc

Address
Av. Rodolfo Neri Vela s/n,
Col. Bosque de Chapultepec
II Sección

Metro
Constituyentes Station, Line 7

Ecobici
CE-711

Hours
Tue-Sun 10:00 - 17:00 h

Entry
Paid admission, free on Sundays

Did you know...?
For years, water from the Lerma system ran directly over Rivera's mural, integrating the work into the actual functioning of the sump.

In the second section of the Bosque de Chapultepec, the Fuente de Tláloc and the Cárcamo de Dolores form a hydraulic and artistic complex key to the urban history of Mexico City. Designed between 1950 and 1951 by architect Ricardo Rivas and muralist Diego Rivera, they were integrated into the Lerma water supply system and the forest landscape as an emblem of post-revolutionary public art. The Cárcamo was built as a distribution chamber connected to the tunnels carrying water to the west of the city. Rivera conceived the complex as a symbolic unit: the monumental fountain with the figure of Tláloc and the interior mural *El agua, origen de la vida*, intended for water to circulate over the painted surface. Continuous use caused its deterioration, so restoration work was undertaken at the end of the twentieth century. In 2010, it reopened as an underground museum dedicated to the link between water, art, and infrastructure.

90

Casa Ortega / Casa Estudio Luis Barragán

Address
Gral. Francisco Ramírez 22 / 12,
Col. Ampliación Daniel Garza

Metro
Constituyentes Station, Line 7

Hours
Casa Ortega Mon-Fri 10:00 - 14:00 h
Casa Estudio Mon-Sat 11:00 - 16:00 h

Entry
Paid admission with prior registration

Did you know...?
Luis Barragán is recognized as the only Mexican architect to have won the Pritzker Prize, in 1980.

Designed, built, and inhabited by Barragán between 1942 and 1947, Casa Ortega was his first house in Mexico City. Inspired by the *haciendas* of his childhood in Jalisco, it reveals an experimental and introspective Barragán and is distinguished by its spacious garden. Next to Casa Ortega, the Casa Estudio—one of the most significant residences of modern international architecture—was built in 1948 and conceived as both a home and professional studio. Today, it is one of the few contemporary properties inscribed on the UNESCO World Heritage List (2004). Both houses present a discreet, almost anonymous facade toward the street, contrasted with an interior of great spatial complexity. Barragán combined elements of Mexican vernacular architecture—solid walls, courtyards, latticework, handcrafted furniture—with principles of European rationalism and a particular attention to light, color, proportion, and silence.

91

Lago Mayor

Did you know...?
The Lago Mayor was built between 1898 and 1900 as a Porfirian landscape work, inspired by European parks and originally conceived for boat rides and public education.

92

Lago Menor

Address
Col. Bosque de Chapultepec II Sección
Metro
Constituyentes Station, Line 7
Metrobús
Campo Marte Station, Line 7
Cablebús
Panteón de Dolores Station, Line 3
Ecobici
CE-711
Hours
Tue-Sun 9:00 - 16:30 h

The Lago Mayor of Chapultepec is one of the widest bodies of water in the forest, a key piece of the landscape and environmental memory of the second section. Its existence recalls the original hydraulic character of Chapultepec, where springs and canals fed both the forest and the ancient Mexico City. With its open mirror of water and tree-lined edge, the lake is today a space for rowing, walking, and contemplating the environment. Interventions by the Chapultepec: Naturaleza y Cultura project have improved water quality, reinforced slopes, and restored paths, recovering essential ecological functions. To the southwest lies the Lago Menor, more intimate and silent, framed by green areas. On its bank stands the Museo de Historia Natural, an emblem of Mexican modernism and an educational reference. Both lakes reflect recent efforts to restore native flora, clean channels, and offer pedestrian and cycling routes that respect wildlife.

93

Lago Algo

Did you know...?
The building was originally the restaurant "El Lago," inaugurated in 1964 as a modernist icon designed by Leónides Guadarrama and Alfonso Ramírez Ponce.

Address
Pista El Sope s/n,
Col. Bosque de Chapultepec
II Sección
Metro
Auditorio Station, Line 7
Cablebús
Los Pinos / Constituyentes Station, Line 3
Ecobici
CE-711
Hours
Tue-Sun 8:30 - 16:30 h

Lago Algo is one of the most relevant cultural spaces in the second section of the Bosque de Chapultepec. Conceived as a contemporary art gallery, the venue occupies a modernist building rehabilitated to integrate into the forest's cultural and environmental corridor. Its architecture, with large windows and a structure that seems to float over the water, establishes a direct dialogue between the exhibited pieces and the landscape of the Lago Mayor. The interior was reinterpreted with a sober, luminous, and flexible aesthetic allowing for installations, temporary exhibitions, and site-specific projects. In this space, art expands toward the natural surroundings, converting the lacustrine landscape into part of the museographic experience. In parallel, Lago Algo functions as a restaurant with a culinary proposal based on local and seasonal ingredients, reinforcing its character as a meeting point for contemporary culture. As an active gallery, Lago Algo exemplifies the renovation of Chapultepec: emblematic properties rehabilitated and returned to the public as creative, accessible, and socially significant spaces.

94

Aztlán Parque Urbano
(Aztlán Feria de Chapultepec)

Address
Av. de los Compositores s/n,
Col. Bosque de Chapultepec
II Sección
Metro
Constituyentes Station,
Line 7
Ecobici
CE-711
Hours
Tue-Sun 12:00 - 20:00 h

Did you know...?
The Aztlán 360 ferris wheel is 85 m high and is considered the largest in Mexico, and is visible from across the city.

The Aztlán Parque Urbano is a space for entertainment, culture, and urban memory built on the former grounds of the Feria de Chapultepec. Inaugurated in 2024, it marks a new stage in Mexico City's amusement parks, under a hybrid model combining mechanical rides, artistic installations, museum architecture, and green areas. For decades, the Feria de Chapultepec was an emblematic site for family leisure, inaugurated in 1964 as part of the modern development of the second section. After it was shut down 2019, the City Government promoted an international call for its transformation. Aztlán was conceived as a space articulating technology, history, sustainability, and urban culture; its name refers to the mythical city of origin of the Mexicas. Among its main attractions stand out a high-altitude ferris wheel, new-generation mechanical rides, an interactive city museum, and scenographic recreations of Tenochtitlan.

95

Papalote Museo del Niño

Address
Av. de los Compositores 710, Col. Bosque de Chapultepec II Sección

Metro
Constituyentes Station, Line 7

Ecobici
CE-711

Hours
Tue-Fri 10:00 - 18:00 h
Sat-Sun 10:00 - 19:00 h

Entry
Paid admission

Did you know...?
The Papalote was one of the first museums in Latin America to have an educational IMAX room, with science and nature projections on a wraparound screen.

The Papalote Museo del Niño is one of the most recognized educational and recreational spaces in Mexico, dedicated to interactive learning for children and teenagers. Inaugurated in 1993, it was a pioneer in the country in the use of participatory museography, combining science, technology, art, and the environment in a setting designed for learning through direct experience. The idea of creating a museum specifically aimed at children took shape in the late 1980s, promoted by the Fundación Papalote with support from public and private institutions. The building was designed by architect Ricardo Legorreta, who resorted to simple geometric forms, intense color, and natural light to create an accessible and stimulating space. With more than 40,000 m^2, the museum integrates interactive halls, outdoor areas, a sustainable garden, an IMAX projection room, and creativity laboratories. Its motto, "Touch, play, and learn," synthesizes a proposal centered on curiosity, with exhibitions addressing topics such as climate change, the human body, water, digital technology, or food culture.

96

Parque Ecológico / Centro de Cultura Ambiental (CCA)

Did you know...?
The park's wetlands were designed to replicate the flows of the ancient lakes of the Basin of Mexico, filtering water through natural processes inspired by pre-Hispanic ecosystems.

Address
Av. de los Compositores s/n, Col. Bosque de Chapultepec II Sección
Metro
Constituyentes Station, Line 7
Cablebús
Los Pinos / Constituyentes Station, Line 3
Ecobici
CE-711
Hours
Mon-Sun 9:00 - 17:00 h

The Parque Ecológico y Centro de Cultura Ambiental is one of the most representative projects of the ecological and cultural renovation of Chapultepec in the twenty-first century. Integrated into the Chapultepec: Naturaleza y Cultura program, it articulates conservation, education, and community participation in a complex spanning the second and third sections of the forest. Its design privileges open terraces, ecological paths, and spaces without visual barriers, built with low-impact materials such as compacted earth, volcanic stone, and certified wood. The park incorporates restored wetlands, pollinator gardens, and environmental interpretation areas explaining the functioning of water, soils, and the valley's biodiversity. The discreet architecture, with light pavilions and natural ventilation, avoids imposing itself on the landscape and reinforces understanding of the environment. The Centro de Cultura Ambiental complements the tour with workshops, exhibitions, conferences, and community programs dedicated to sustainability, energy transition, and the rights of nature.

97

Museo de Historial Natural y Cultura Ambiental

Address
Av. de los Compositores s/n, Col. Bosque de Chapultepec II Sección

Metro
Constituyentes Station, Line 7

Hours
Tue-Sun 10:00 - 17:00 h

Entry
Paid admission, free on Sundays

Did you know...?
A real meteorite, is on display in the central lobby—one of the oldest rocks visible in the country.

This museum is a scientific and educational institution dedicated to disseminating knowledge about the evolution of the universe, the Earth, and life. Since its opening, it has taken on the mission of bringing geological, biological, and cosmic processes closer to the public. The design, by Leónides Guadarrama, is organized into galleries and domes, and its thematic focus make it an accessible space for children, teenagers, and the general public. The museum has antecedents in scientific collections from the late nineteenth century, but its current configuration responds to the modern urban project of Chapultepec's second section. Its exhibitions combine dioramas, three-dimensional models, fossils, multimedia resources, and interactive modules. Remodeled on several occasions, most recently between 2017 and 2020, it has incorporated new technologies and sustainability standards.

98

Parque de Cultura Urbana (PARCUR)

99

Serpiente y escaleras

Did you know...?
This space operated as a water park until it was abandoned in 2007. After many years, it was restored and can now be visited.

Tercera Sección del Bosque de Chapultepec

The third section of the Bosque de Chapultepec is the most serene and expansive zone of the park: less crowded and wider. In recent years, this territory was integrated into the PARCUR program, a recreational corridor recovering green spaces, improving pedestrian mobility, and creating clear routes for walking, running, or cycling without losing the feeling of being in a natural environment.

100

Panteón Civil Dolores

Address
Av. Ignacio Zaragoza 224,
Col. Bosque de Chapultepec
III Sección
Cablebús
Panteón de Dolores Station,
PARCUR / Colegio de Arquitectos
Station, Line 3
Hours
Tue-Sun 6:00 - 18:00 h

Recent interventions incorporated paths and rest areas distributed among hills, clearings, and wooded stretches. Standing out here is Serpientes y Escaleras, a system of paths inspired by the traditional board game (Sankes and Ladders). It does not replicate boards or colors: its playful nod appears in the way it takes advantage of slopes, landings, and viewpoints to guide the visitor without altering the wild character of the area. The third section maintains its vocation for exploration, and to the west, the corridor links naturally with the historical environment of the Panteón Civil de Dolores, expanding the experience toward a heritage landscape. Together, the third section, PARCUR, and Serpientes y Escaleras form an ideal corridor to discover a lesser-known, freer, and fully walkable Chapultepec.

101

Cineteca Nacional Chapultepec

Address
Av. Vasco de Quiroga 1401, Col. Santa Fe
Cablebús
Cineteca Chapultepec / Bodega de Arte Station, Line 3
Hours
Mon-Sun 11:30 - 18:00 h

Did you know...?
This space constitutes the fourth section of the forest, an area that during the twentieth century belonged to the Secretaría de la Defensa Nacional and was later transferred for its conservation.

Cuarta Sección del Bosque de Chapultepec

The fourth section of the Bosque de Chapultepec has acquired a central role in the cultural life of the city's west thanks to two key projects: the Cablebús Line 3 and the new Cineteca Nacional Chapultepec. The Cablebús, inaugurated in July 2024, transformed the forest's connectivity by linking its four sections through a 5 km aerial corridor running from Los Pinos / Constituyentes Station to Vasco de Quiroga

102

Cablebús Chapultepec

149 Station, connecting with the Tren Interurbano. In addition to functioning as public transport—accessible with the Tarjeta de Movilidad Integrada (MI)—it offers a panoramic tour flying over previously inaccessible areas and directly articulates the third and fourth sections within the Chapultepec: Naturaleza y Cultura project. Its cabins feature universal accessibility, and the complete journey takes approximately twenty-one minutes. In this new cultural circuit, the Cineteca Nacional Chapultepec stands out: an open and accessible space surrounded by green areas. Its modern halls, open-air screenings, and surrounding walkways make it a natural meeting point for both visitors and locals. With both projects, the fourth section consolidates itself as a corridor where mobility, culture, and landscape integrate organically.

5

During the second half of the twentieth century, Zona Rosa became a key transitional space in the urban and social history of Mexico City. Its streets, originally laid out during the Porfiriato (1876–1911), were transformed into settings of modernity, rupture, and cultural experimentation. The remnants of the area's former French-inspired elegance coexisted with an increasingly diverse social life that challenged the moral limits of the postrevolutionary regime. Bars, cafés, cabarets, cantinas, and nightclubs shaped a new face of the city—one that was more cosmopolitan and open to the political, artistic, and social transformations of the twentieth century.

Zona Rosa

Between the 1960s and 1970s, Zona Rosa reached its peak as a bohemian center and enclave of the capital's intellectual community. Writers, artists, diplomats, students, and journalists turned the neighborhood into a meeting point. In a context marked by growing authoritarianism in the mid-twentieth century, Zona Rosa offered refuge to alternative expressions that found no place in institutional circuits. It served as a release valve and, at the same time, as an urban laboratory where new forms of identity and community emerged.

Its bars provided something scarce at the time: anonymity, belonging, and freedom. Yet, this atmosphere of openness coexisted with censorship and repression. Police raids, institutional discrimination, and social stigma persisted, but forms of resistance also emerged, later contributing to social movements and new rights. Within this territory, some of the first support networks, information centers, and collectives took shape, making visible other ways of inhabiting the city.

Over time, Zona Rosa changed once again. Real-estate pressure, the area's increasing complexity, and the shift of nightlife to other districts altered its original character. Even so, its streets preserve the memory of a decisive moment of openness and diversity. More than a district devoted to leisure, it was a space of encounter and dissent. Zona Rosa contributed—through everyday life and cultural exchange—to widening the boundaries of freedom in Mexico City.

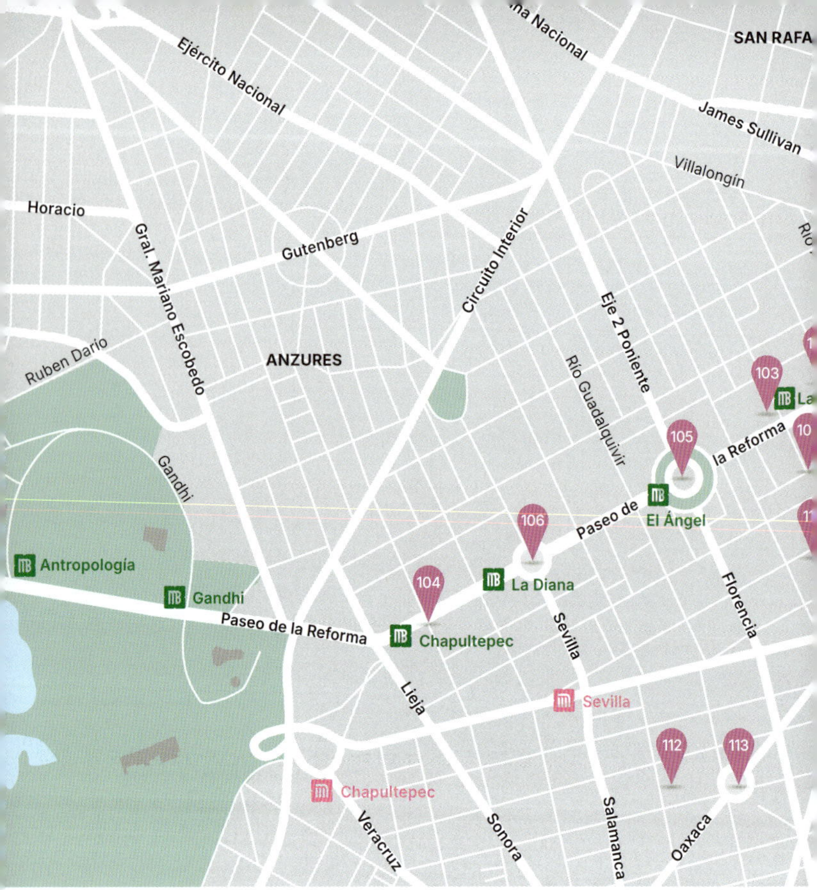

Route 5 / Zona Rosa

103 Paseo de la Reforma

104 The four towers

105 Monumento de la Independencia

106 Fuente de la Diana Cazadora

107 Parroquia de la Votiva

108 Reforma 222

109 Museo de la Bolsa Mexicana de Valores (MUBO)

110 Hotel Geneve

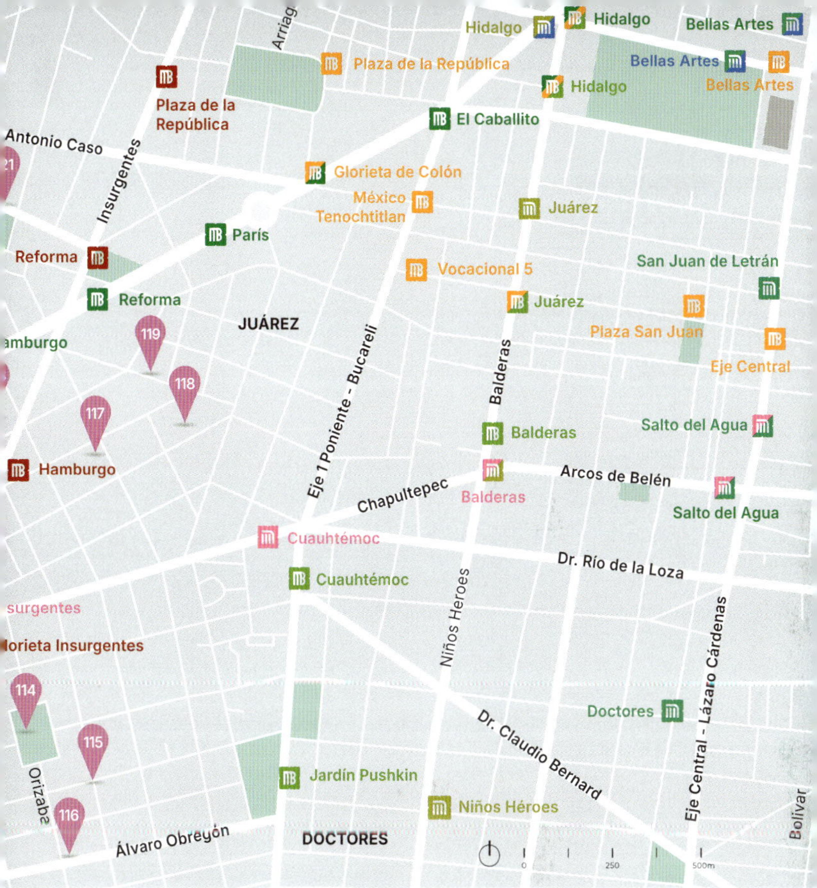

111 Glorieta de los Insurgentes

112 Casa Museo Guillermo Tovar de Teresa

113 Fuente de Cibeles

114 Plaza Río de Janeiro

115 Museo del Objeto del Objeto (MODO)

116 Centro Cultural Casa Lamm

117 Plaza Washington

118 Museo Ripley / Museo de Cera

119 Museo del Chocolate (MUCHO)

120 Museo Casa de Carranza

121 Museo Experimental El Eco

103

Paseo de la Reforma

Did you know...?
For decades, the Glorieta de la Palma housed a centennial Canary Island date palm that became a symbol of the city. After its removal due to plant disease, an ahuehuete tree was planted as a symbol of the region's endemic flora.

Address
From Chapultepec to Centro Histórico
Metro
Chapultepec Station, Sevilla Station, and Insurgentes Station, Line 1
Metrobús
Chapultepec, La Diana, El Ángel, El Ahuehuete, Hamburgo and Reforma Stations, Line 7
Ecobici
CE-014, CE-013, CE-261, CE-022, CE-021, CE-015, CE-023, CE-016, CE-024, CE-017, CE-025, CE-018, CE-019, CE-027

With more than 14 km in length, Paseo de la Reforma is one of the most emblematic avenues in Mexico City, due to both its urban layout and its historical and symbolic relevance. Conceived in 1864 by order of Emperor Maximilian of Habsburg to connect the Castillo de Chapultepec with the city, it was originally named *Paseo de la Emperatriz*. After the end of the second empire, it adopted its current name, alluding to the Reform Laws. Inspired by the boulevards of Paris and Vienna, this roadway was designed as a tree-lined imperial promenade that eventually transformed into the capital's main axis. Throughout the twentieth century, Reforma was modernized with the insertion of skyscrapers, embassies, and public spaces. It has been the object of successive revitalizations that incorporated bicycle lanes, sculptural gardens, and pedestrian areas. Today, it is a corridor where history, political power, urban life, and collective memory converge.

104

The four towers

Did you know...?
Torre Reforma has LEED Platinum certification and a seismic design based on two reinforced concrete lateral walls that act as "wings." The base of the Torre Reforma integrates a Porfirian large house (*casona*) preserved as part of the original property.

Torre Reforma
Av. Paseo de la Reforma 483,
Col. Cuauhtémoc
Torre BBVA
Av. Paseo de la Reforma 510,
Col. Juárez
Torre Mayor
Av. Paseo de la Reforma 505,
Col. Cuauhtémoc
Torre Chapultepec Uno R509
Río Ródano 509,
Col. Cuauhtémoc
Metro
Sevilla Station, Line 1
Metrobús
Chapultepec Station, Line 7
Ecobici
CE-007, CE-014, CE-028

The Torre Reforma, Torre BBVA, Torre Mayor, and Torre Chapultepec Uno towers make up one of the most representative architectural and financial nodes of Paseo de la Reforma, a corridor that has accompanied the urban transformation of Mexico City in recent decades. This group of skyscrapers evidences the consolidation of a vertical front that gradually replaced the old Porfirian avenue of small palaces and today expresses the country's technical, economic, and urban planning capabilities. Torre Reforma, at 246 m in height—LBR & Arquitectos—, obtained the international recognition "Best Tall Building Worldwide" in 2018, awarded by the Council on Tall Buildings and Urban Habitat. The Torre BBVA—Legorreta® and Rogers Stirk Harbour + Partners—, built of steel, concrete, and metal profiles, reaches the height of the Torre Mayor—Zeidler Roberts Partnership and Reichmann International—at 225 m, directly on the other side of Paseo de la Reforma. Torre Chapultepec Uno—ARQUITECTOMA—, at 241 m in height with its glass facade, is one of the largest mixed-use complexes in the country.

105

Monumento de la Independencia

Address
Av. Paseo de la Reforma 342, Col. Juárez
Metro
Insurgentes Station, Line 1
Metrobús
El Ángel Station, Line 7
Ecobici
CE-016, CE-017, CE-024, CE-025

Did you know...?
During the 1957 earthquake, the sculpture of the Angel fell from its pedestal and broke into several parts. It was meticulously restored and reinforced before being repositioned months later. Since then, its structure has been constantly monitored.

The Monumento a la Independencia, popularly known as "El Ángel," is one of the most recognizable symbols of Mexico City. The golden figure of a Winged Victory that crowns the column, symbolizes triumph and freedom. It was inaugurated in 1910 as part of the Centennial of Independence celebrations during the government of Porfirio Díaz. Although its image is associated with national identity today, its history is deeply linked to the political context of the Porfiriato and the ideals of progress and modernity that marked the beginning of the twentieth century. Since then, the monument has been the stage for official tributes, social demonstrations, and popular celebrations, becoming an emblematic meeting point for the country's public life. The project was designed by architect Antonio Rivas Mercado, with sculptures by the Italian Enrique Alciati, author of the allegorical figures and bronze reliefs that decorate the base.
The construction faced technical difficulties due to soil instability, which forced the foundation to be rebuilt almost entirely.
Work began in 1902 and, after several delays, was concluded and inaugurated eight years later.
At its base lie the remains of the main heroes of Independence —Miguel Hidalgo, José María Morelos, Vicente Guerrero, among others—transferred there in 1925. This funerary space, civic and solemn in character, reinforces its role as a national monument. Throughout the twentieth century, the monument has withstood earthquakes, restorations, and urban transformations, remaining one of the most enduring images of modern Mexican history.

106

Fuente de la Diana Cazadora

Address
Av. Paseo de la Reforma and Sevilla, Col. Juárez
Metro
Sevilla Station, Line 1
Metrobús
La Diana Station, Line 7
Ecobici
CE-013, CE-021, CE-022, CE-023, CE-015

Did you know...?
The identity of the model for the Diana Cazadora, Helvia Martínez, was kept in secret for decades by official decision, which generated public curiosity and multiple speculations at the time.

This site is one of the most recognizable landmarks of Paseo de la Reforma and a reference point for modern urbanism in Mexico City. Inaugurated in 1942, it integrates the sculpture by Juan Fernando Olaguíbel and the architectural project by Vicente Mendiola into a piece that articulates art, landscape, and monumental scale on this central avenue. The main figure, originally called *The Archer of the Northern Stars*, represents the goddess Diana drawing her bow. The work generated debate from its installation due to its nudity, which led to the addition of a bronze loincloth that eventually damaged the piece. This deterioration motivated its replacement by the replica that occupies the roundabout today, while the original sculpture was moved to Ixmiquilpan, Hidalgo. After various movements due to roadworks, the fountain was reinstalled in its current location in 1992, where it once again integrated into the urban landscape as a reference point and identity of the Reforma corridor.

107

Parroquia de la Votiva

Address
Av. Paseo de la Reforma 290, Col. Juárez
Metro
Insurgentes Station, Line 1
Metrobús
Ahuehuete Station, Line 7
Hours
Tue-Sun 10:00 - 18:00 h
Ecobici
CE-018

Did you know...?
This is the only church that survived Reforma's original layout.

The origin of this temple, built during the first half of the twentieth century, is linked to the vow made by Father Luis G. Romo, who, after witnessing the destruction of a church during the Revolution, promised to dedicate a temple to the Sacred Heart in the capital. The project was led by architect Francisco Martínez Gallardo, with the technical collaboration of Ernesto Gómez Arzapalo on the foundation. While construction progressed, a provisional chapel was enabled and began functioning in 1922.

In architectural terms, La Votiva features a facade with discreet ornaments and a simple interior oriented towards devotion to the Sacred Heart, with a high altar that structures the nave and favors contemplation. Today, it maintains constant activity through masses, sacraments, and moments of community prayer. Its presence on Reforma integrates it into the group of temples that document the urban and cultural transformation of this part of the city, forming part of the corridor's architectural and cultural heritage.

108

Reforma 222

Address
Av. Paseo de la Reforma 222, Col. Juárez
Metro
Insurgentes Station, Line 1
Metrobús
Hamburgo Station, Lines 1 and 7
Cuauhtémoc Station, Line 3
Ecobici
CE-027
Hours
Mon-Sun 11:00 - 20:00 h

Did you know...?
The shopping center in this mixed-used building was conceived as a covered street, with natural ventilation and visual interaction between levels, inspired by the principles of an open city.

Designed by architect Teodoro González de León and inaugurated in 2007, this mixed-use architectural complex integrates housing, offices, and commerce into a single complex. Its design privileges interaction between public space and contemporary architecture through pedestrian access, terraces, and an open commercial gallery.
It is one of the projects that consolidated the new urban profile of Reforma in the twenty-first century, contributing to the revitalization of a previously deteriorated area. The complex stands out for its balance between functionality, aesthetics, and openness to the surroundings. During the first decades of the twenty-first century, Paseo de la Reforma was the object of diverse renovation projects, and Reforma 222 became one of the most ambitious.
It occupies an entire block and is composed of three towers —two residential and one for offices—in addition to an open-plan shopping center.

109

Museo de la Bolsa Mexicana de Valores (MUBO)

Did you know...?
The dome crowning the Bolsa Mexicana de Valores—visible from Paseo de la Reforma—is a circular LED screen of more than 200 m² where quotes and institutional messages are projected.

Address
Av. Paseo de la Reforma 255, Col. Cuauhtémoc
Metro
Insurgentes Station, Line 1
Metrobús
El Ahuehuete Station, Line 7
Ecobici
CE-018
Hours
Mon-Fri 9:00 - 17:00 h
Sun 10:00 - 15:00 h
Entry
Free admission

Located inside the Bolsa Mexicana de Valores building, this museum offers a didactic and visual journey through the evolution of financial markets in Mexico, from pre-Hispanic barter to the digital transactions of the twenty-first century. Inaugurated in 2010, it is part of the Institution's efforts to promote financial education and bring the public closer to the stock market world. Its halls exhibit models, historical documents, interactive screens, real-time graphics, old banknotes, and stock securities, as well as a recreation of the old trading floor. The tour integrates not only technical aspects but also the social, political, and economic contexts that have marked Mexican markets: inflationary crises, trade openness, and financial globalization. The Bolsa Mexicana de Valores operated for decades in the Centro Histórico. Its current building by Juan José Díaz Infante and inaugurated in 1990 with its distinctive metallic dome, houses both the headquarters and the museum. One of the most attractive points is the visual access to the digital trading floor, where market fluctuations are projected in real time.

110

Hotel Geneve

Address
Londres 130, Col. Juárez
Metro
Insurgentes Station, Line 1
Metrobús
Insurgentes Station, Line 1
Ecobici
CE-034, CE-035

Did you know...?
The Phone Bar at the Hotel Geneve displays a collection of antique telephones and period objects that illustrate the hotel's pioneering role in the modernization of services and the evolution of telecommunications in the country.

Inaugurated in 1907, it is one of the oldest and most representative lodgings in Mexico City. Conceived as a luxury hotel in the European style, it was a pioneer in incorporating innovations such as a telephone in every room, heating, elevators, and multilingual staff. Its eclectic architecture, with neoclassical and *art nouveau* influences, reflects the cosmopolitan spirit of the Porfiriato. Throughout the twentieth century, it witnessed key episodes in the country's political, diplomatic, and cultural life. Since its early years, the Hotel Geneve was a meeting point for diplomats, writers, and political leaders. Notable visitors include Porfirio Díaz, Winston Churchill, Charles Lindbergh, and Gabriel García Márquez. During the Mexican Revolution, its bar was known as "the bar of intrigues" due to the meetings it hosted between spies, correspondents, and expatriates. Its proximity to embassies, government offices, and newsrooms made it a nerve center for information and discretion. Still in operation, it preserves much of its original furniture and houses a small museum that documents its history.

111

Glorieta de los Insurgentes

Address
Av. Insurgentes Sur and Av. Chapultepec, Col. Roma
Metro
Insurgentes Station, Line 1
Metrobús
Insurgentes Station, Line 1
Ecobici
CE-034, CE-035

Did you know...?
In March 2008, the famous confrontation between emos and punks at the Glorieta de Insurgentes was contained by Hare Krishna members and the police.

This roundabout, which articulates the connection between Insurgentes, Chapultepec, and the access points to Roma Norte, Colonia Juárez, and the Zona Rosa, is one of the busiest urban nodes in Mexico City. Built in 1969 within a transit modernization project, it was inaugurated alongside the first Metro line. The design, led by architect Salvador Ortega, transformed a traditional neighborhood-scale crossing—previously surrounded by Porfirian houses—into a monumental rotunda capable of absorbing the growing flow of an expanding city. The project implied the demolition of old buildings and the creation of a vehicular ring accompanied by an elevated pedestrian platform and underground passages that integrated access to the Metro, commercial premises, and different circulation levels. Over time, the environment grew in density and activity, consolidating the roundabout as a key point for mobility, commerce, and daily life in the area, as well as a reference for the urban development of the second half of the twentieth century.

112

Casa Museo Guillermo Tovar de Teresa

Address
Valladolid 52,
Col. Roma Norte
Metro
Sevilla Station, Line 1
Metrobús
Álvaro Obregón Station, Line 1
Ecobici
CE-042
Hours
Mon-Sun 10:30 - 17:00 h
Entry
Free admission

Did you know...?
Guillermo Tovar lived without a computer or cell phone. He wrote by hand and dictated his letters to a typewriter, surrounded by art and silence. A childhood portrait painted by Ignacio Barrios is preserved in his main living room.

Located in a Porfirian *casona* in Colonia Roma Norte, the Casa Museo Guillermo Tovar de Teresa was the residence of historian and bibliophile Guillermo Tovar de Teresa (1956-2013), one of the most notable figures in the conservation of twentieth-century Mexican cultural heritage. Since its opening in 2018, the museum has offered an intimate journey through the life, work, and collection of the man considered the last Mexican humanist in the classical sense. The building, constructed around 1911, preserves stained glass, ironwork, marble, tapestries, and historical furniture that frame the collection gathered by Tovar: viceregal paintings, nineteenth-century art, documents, portraits, sculptures, sacred art, and photographs. Each room was preserved according to its original use, maintaining the researcher's domestic atmosphere. The museum houses a library specializing in Mexican history and art, as well as a personal archive. Managed by the Fundación Carlos Slim, the venue pays tribute to the intellectual rigor and patrimonial vocation of Tovar, a member of the Academia Mexicana de la Historia and official chronicler of Mexico City.

Fuente de Cibeles

Address
Plaza Villa de Madrid, Col. Roma Norte
Metro
Sevilla Station, Line 1
Metrobús
Insurgentes Station, Line 1
Ecobici
CE-047

Did you know...?
During its installation, Spanish technicians traveled to supervise the reproduction to ensure that the proportions were faithful to the original fountain, which made this piece one of the most precise replicas outside Spain.

As a reference point in Colonia Roma, this fountain is an almost an exact replica of the one installed in the Plaza de Cibeles in Madrid. Donated in 1980 by the Spanish community residing in Mexico as a gesture of friendship between both nations, it reproduces the image of the goddess Cybele on a chariot pulled by two lions, a classical motif from Greco-Roman mythology that has naturally integrated into the urban landscape.

The space where it is located was designed as a roundabout that articulates several important streets, granting it a relevant role in the urban reading of the area. Over time, the fountain has acquired its own cultural meaning: it functions as a meeting point, a landmark, and a frequent stage for celebrations linked to the Spanish community and visitors touring Roma.

114

Plaza Río de Janeiro

Address
Plaza Río de Janeiro 54,
Col. Roma Norte
Metro
Insurgentes Station, Line 1
Metrobús
Durango Station, Line 1
Ecobici
CE-128

Did you know...?
The name change to "Río de Janeiro," carried out in 1922, surprised the area's first inhabitants. Over time, the new denomination was fully integrated and today forms part of the historical identity of the plaza.

Today one of the most representative green spaces in Roma, this plaza was created in 1903 as part of the colony's first developments. Its design was integrated into the Porfirian urban project that sought to incorporate green areas and walking spaces within a modern residential environment. The layout of the plaza, defined by the crossing of Durango and Orizaba streets, responded to the intention of balancing architecture and public life in the new neighborhood. The place received different names—Parque Roma and Parque Orizaba—before adopting the current one in 1922, when Mexico recognized the centennial of Brazil's independence. Since then, it has consolidated itself as an identity point for the neighborhood. In its center stands a circular fountain with a bronze replica of Michelangelo's David, installed in 1976 during a remodeling of the surroundings. Among the buildings surrounding it, the Edificio Río de Janeiro stands out, known as the Witch House, built in 1908 and distinguished by its singular silhouette. Today, the plaza functions as a daily meeting point for residents and visitors.

115

Museo del Objeto del Objeto (MODO)

Did you know...?
The name of the museum points to the multiple ways objects can be interpreted: as things, but also as vehicles of memory, design, industry, and desire.

Address
Colima 145,
Col. Roma Norte
Metro
Insurgentes Station, Line 1
Metrobús
Durango Station, Line 1
Ecobici
CE-130
Hours
Tue-Sun 10:00 - 18:00 h
Entry
Paid admission

Located in a Porfirian *casona* from the early twentieth century, the building was carefully restored to house this museum dedicated to the study of design, communication, and material culture. Founded in 2010 by Bruno Newman, a collector and communicator, it safeguards more than 140,000 objects covering more than two centuries of the history of consumption, daily life, and visual languages in Mexico. From packaging, labels, transport tickets, old radios, and toys to posters, advertisements, and political campaign objects, the collection allows for tracing the history of the everyday, with one of the most important archives of its kind in Latin America. The museum does not have a permanent exhibition; its focus is curatorial and thematic, organizing each temporary show as a narrative constructed from objects selected with historical rigor and visual sense. Additionally, the MODO functions as a research center for graphic and industrial design in Mexico and has contributed to the conservation of pieces previously not considered heritage.

116

Centro Cultural Casa Lamm

Address
Av. Álvaro Obregón 99,
Col. Roma Norte

Metrobús
Jardín Pushkin Station, Line 3

Ecobici
CE-134

Hours
Mon-Fri 8:00 - 19:00 h
Sat 10:00 - 13:00 h

Did you know...?
The house was never inhabited by the Lamm family, for whom it was originally built. Its subsequent preservation allowed for the conservation of one of the few intact Porfirian residential examples in Roma, despite demolitions during the twentieth century.

Built in 1911, this Porfirian residence is part of the early development of Colonia Roma as a modern residential zone inspired by European models. Its eclectic architecture, with French influences and ornamental details typical of the period, reflects the urban ideal that marked the consolidation of the colony at the beginning of the twentieth century. Despite being conceived as a residence for Lewis Lamm, the house was first occupied by the Marist Brothers, who established the headquarters of the Colegio Francés Jalisco there. Later, it passed to the García Collantes family, who kept it during a large part of the twentieth century and prevented its demolition in a period of strong urban transformations. In 1993, a comprehensive restoration process began that allowed for the recovery of its architectural value. A year later, it reopened as the Centro Cultural Casa Lamm dedicated to cultural training and dissemination. The venue houses galleries, exhibition halls, spaces for publishing presentations, and a wide academic offer. Its gardens and interior courtyards complement a complex that articulates historical architecture and contemporary cultural life.

117

Plaza Washington

Address
Dinamarca 42-30,
Col. Juárez
Metro
Cuauhtémoc Station, Line 1
Metrobús
Hamburgo Station, Lines 1 and 7
Ecobici
CE-118

Did you know...?
The plaza retains its original Porfirian layout and formerly hosted old diplomatic headquarters in its surroundings; later, it became a meeting point for the first artistic communities that occupied the Colonia Juárez.

This plaza stands out for its circular layout, its mature trees, and its relationship with the Porfirian trace that defined the urban project of the late nineteenth century. Designed as part of an orderly extension of Paseo de la Reforma, it functions as a node that articulates residential and commercial streets and allows for recognizing the transition between Porfirian mansions, twentieth-century functionalist buildings, and contemporary interventions in the colony. The space operates as a neighborhood meeting point, a corridor for passing through, and a resting site within an area marked by the mixture of housing, offices, galleries, and restoration. Its permanence condenses the historical identity of the Juárez neighborhood, a colony affected by earthquakes, abandonment, and renewal processes, that still preserves key urban pieces to understand the city's growth beyond the Centro Histórico. Visiting the plaza reveals how foreign urban models were adopted while the neighborhood's human-scale qualities were preserved.

118

Museo Ripley / Museo de Cera

Did you know...?
Both museums occupy historical mansions of Colonia Juárez: one designed to evoke castles and another built between 1900 and 1904, which makes architecture an essential part of the visit experience.

Address
Londres 4 and Londres 6, Col. Juárez

Metro
Cuauhtémoc Station, Line 1

Metrobús
Hamburgo Station, Lines 1 and 7
Cuauhtémoc Station, Line 3

Ecobici
CE-116

Hours
Mon-Sun 11:00 - 19:00 h

Entry
Paid admission

The Museo Ripley and the Museo de Cera make up a set of attractions installed in historical mansions. Inaugurated in 1992, the Museo Ripley forms part of the international franchise *Believe It or Not!* and stands out for its playful approach. It exhibits more than 200 pieces including anthropological rarities, unusual objects, and documented phenomena, organized in 14 thematic rooms that revisit the exploratory curiosity of Robert L. Ripley. Its building, designed to evoke medieval castles and Victorian styles, seeks to provoke amazement from the entrance. The Museo de Cera, opened in 1979, is located inside a large house built between 1900 and 1904, representative of residential architecture from the beginning of the twentieth century. This building adds heritage value to the museum, making it not only an exhibition space but also a testimony to the area's urban history. Its collection exceeds 200 figures distributed in thematic rooms that are updated periodically.

119

Museo del Chocolate (MUCHO)

Did you know...?
The word *chocolate* comes from the Nahuatl *xocolatl*, which means "bitter water." In the Mexica era, cacao was also used as a currency of exchange.

Address
Milán 45,
Col. Juárez
Metro
Cuauhtémoc Station, Line 1
Metrobús
Reforma Station, Line 7
Hamburgo Station, Lines 1 and 7
Ecobici
CE-116
Hours
Mon-Sun 11:00 - 17:00 h
Entry
Paid admission

Located in a Porfirian mansion, the MUCHO is a cultural and sensory space dedicated to the history, tradition, and science of cacao, a food originating in Mesoamerica. Founded in 2012 as an independent initiative, the museum proposes an immersive experience to understand the central role of chocolate in the history of Mexico and its global projection. The headquarters, restored to its original elements—wood floors, stained glass, stairs, and balconies—offers a journey that goes from the ritual use of cacao in the Olmec, Maya, and Mexica cultures to its transformation in the European industry and its current role as an object of design, research, and sophisticated consumption. Throughout its rooms, the visitor can observe seeds, utensils, codices, old packaging, and machinery, as well as learn about the grain transformation process. Topics such as fair trade, botanical diversity, and the environmental impact of cultivation are also addressed.

120

Museo Casa de Carranza

Did you know...?
The bed where Carranza slept was moved to Tlaxcalantongo, where he was assassinated. The museum has an exact replica in the president's original bedroom.

Address
Río Lerma 35,
Col. Cuauhtémoc
Metro
Sevilla Station, Line 1
Metrobús
Hamburgo Station, Lines 1 and 7
Ecobici
CE-011
Hours
Mon-Sat 9:00 - 18:00 h
Sun 9:00 - 17:00 h
Entry
Paid admission

This house is a Porfirian mansion converted into a museum in 1961, which safeguards the memory of President Venustiano Carranza, a central figure of Constitutionalism during the Mexican Revolution. The building was his official residence and the last one he inhabited in the capital before fleeing to Veracruz in 1920, following the Agua Prieta uprising. Built at the beginning of the twentieth century, the house reflects the French-influenced tastes of the Porfirian elite: carved quarry facade, stained glass, marbles, high ceilings with decorated soffits, and period furniture. Throughout 13 rooms distributed over two floors, the museum preserves Carranza's personal objects, original documents, photographs, uniforms, and recreations of intimate spaces such as his office and bedroom. The tour allows for understanding the life of the First Chief of the Constitutionalist Army, the process of drafting the 1917 Constitution, and the context of his death in Tlaxcalantongo, Puebla.

121

Museo Experimental El Eco

Address
James Sullivan 43,
Col. San Rafael
Metro
Revolución Station, Line 2
Metrobús
Reforma Station, Line 1
Ecobici
CE-085
Hours
Tue-Sun 11:00 - 18:00 h
Entry
Free admission

Did you know...?
When it opened in the 50's, its programming included free dance, recitations, performances, and experimental actions with animals. These activities made El Eco an unusual artistic laboratory for its time and ahead of contemporary practices.

Designed by Mathias Goeritz, this museum space emerged as part of a search to expand the limits of artistic creation. His proposal, linked to so-called "emotional architecture," shaped a venue where the visitor would experience the space as a work in itself. Construction began in 1952 and the museum opened in 1953 as a place of experimentation for exhibitions, sculpture, dance, music, and interdisciplinary activities. Its architecture —high walls, narrow corridors, and courtyards that modulate light—defined a route designed to generate specific sensations. During the s econd half of the twentieth century, the building had diverse uses, among them a restaurant and a nightclub. In 2004 it was acquired by the UNAM, which undertook a restoration process to recover Goeritz's original vision. Reopened in 2005 and it resumed its vocation as an active artistic laboratory and, since 2010, it has housed the Pabellón Eco, an annual contest for young architects.

6

The history of Mexico City cannot be understood solely from its foundational core. Along the margins of the former Basin of Mexico, territories such as San Ángel, Chimalistac, Coyoacán, and Santa Úrsula Coapa form a corridor where traces of the pre-Hispanic world, the viceregal order, and urban modernity converge. Each of these places preserve fragments of the past that, when brought together, outline a continuous reading of the city.

San Ángel / Estadio

San Ángel—formerly Tenanitla—existed before the conquest as an agricultural settlement on the slopes of the Ajusco—a mountain south of Mexico City—. The eruption of the Xitle volcano in the fourth century CE covered the area with lava, creating the basalt of the Pedregal, which shaped its architecture and cultivation. With the arrival of the Discalced Carmelites, the Convento de El Carmen was founded and today stands as one of the most notable examples of New Spanish conventual Baroque. Its layout, preserves the semi-urban character that defined its landscape for centuries.

Chimalistac, a small enclave between San Ángel and Coyoacán, was once part of the Carmelite lands. Its name, derived from the Náhuatl *chimalli* (shield) and *istac* (white), refers to an ancient neighborhood subordinated to Coyoacán. The latter represents a singular historical node: a pre-Hispanic settlement, the first seat of viceregal government, and a criollo town before its incorporation into the capital. From here, Hernán Cortés organized the construction of the new city after the fall of Tenochtitlan. Its layout, temples, and squares create a space where pre-Hispanic memory and viceregal urban structure intertwine with nineteenth-century intellectual life and the artistic ferment of the twentieth century. It was also home to major artists and thinkers, including Frida Kahlo, Diego Rivera, and Leon Trotsky.

The route continues at the Estadio Banorte, inaugurated in 1966 over the southern lava fields. A symbol of Mexican modernity, its monumental scale transformed the urban landscape, marking the shift from convent to colossus, from volcanic stone to reinforced concrete. Continuing through the center of Tlalpan, a historical enclave rooted in the natural landscape of the southern basin, characterized not only by volcanic soil but also by its cool climate and surrounding high mountains. Once a place of convents, orchards, and open spaces—and the site of the first telephone call made in Mexico—the former San Agustín de las Cuevas, as it was known in the nineteenth century, features architecture adapted to this distinctive corner of the city, one of the best-preserved areas of the metropolis.

Finally, the central campus of the UNAM, Ciudad Universitaria, demonstrates the magnitude of the country's mid-twentieth-century public educational project. Built in the early 1950s, the architectural complex was created by the most distinguished architects, urban planners, muralists, and engineers of the era. Highlights include the murals of the Central Library and the views of the Estadio Olímpico Universitario, within a site designated a UNESCO World Heritage Site.

MIXCOAC
Mixcoac
Eje 7 Sur - Félix Cuevas
Félix Cuevas
Insurgentes Sur
Hospital 20 de Noviembre
Gabriel Mancera
Zapata
Eje 1 Pte. México Coyoacán
Parque de los Venados
División del Norte
Eje Central - Lázaro Cárdenas
Porta
Periférico
Revolución
Circuito Interior - Río Mixcoac
Río Churubusco
Eje 8 Sur - José María Rico
Teatro de los Insurgentes
Universidad
Ermita
Eje 8 Sur - Popocatépetl
Barranca del Muerto
José María Velasco
Coyoacán
Eje Central
Circuito Interior - Río Churubusco
Francia
Hortensia
Minerva
Madrid
Olivo
Viveros
Xicoténcatl
General Anaya
Altavista
Vito Alessio Robles
Diego Rivera
Francisco Sosa
Miguel Hidalgo
Ignacio Allende
Fernández Leal
La Bombilla
Miguel Ángel de Quevedo
Miguel Ángel de Quevedo
Tasque
SAN ÁNGEL
Insurgentes
Calzada Taxq
Pacífico
COYOACÁN
Doctor Gálvez
Eje 10 Sur
Copilco
Eje 10 Sur - Pedro Henríquez Ureña
División de
SANTO DOMINGO
Ciudad Universitaria
Universidad
CIUDAD UNIVERSITARIA
Eje Central Aztecas
Iztaccíhuatl
Mario de La Cueva
Popocatépetl
Centro Cultural Universitario
Papatzin
Insurgentes
Del Imán
Del Imán
SANTA ÚRSULA
Circuito Estadio Azteca
Perisur
Periférico
Villa Olímpica
Calzada de Tlalpan
Camino a Santa Teresa
San Fernando
Corregidora
Ayuntamiento
Miguel Hidalgo
Magisterio Nacional
Periférico
Fuentes Brotantes
Viaducto Tlalpan
Santa Úrsula
122
123
124
125
126
127
128
129
130
131
132
133
134
135
136
137
138
139
140
141
142
143
144
145
146
147
148
149
151
152
153
154
0
250
500m

Route 6 / San Ángel-Estadio

122

Cineteca Nacional de México

Address
Av. México Coyoacán 389,
Col. Xoco
Metro
Station Coyoacán, Line 3
Ecobici
CE-432

Since its foundation in 1974 as the principal center for the preservation and dissemination of cinema in Mexico, this institution has played a decisive role in audience development and the conservation of the country's film memory. Its first headquarters, located at the Estudios Churubusco, brought together exhibition halls and vaults designed to conserve film prints under controlled conditions. From the beginning, it stood out for its programming outside the commercial circuit, becoming a meeting point for cinephiles, researchers, and students. Two years after the fire, a new headquarters opened in the Xoco neighborhood, built originally as Plaza de los Compositores by architect Manuel Rocha in 1984. Over time, the complex incorporated a video library, a gallery, consultation areas, and services capable of meeting research and audiovisual management needs. The expansions carried out in 2012 by Michel Rojkind and Gerardo Salinas transformed the precinct into a cultural complex of reference. Today, it features ten movie theaters, an open-air forum, study and reading areas, a bookstore, and public spaces that integrate cultural activities continuously. Its contemporary architecture, conceived to favor pedestrian circulation and generate open plazas, links the cinematic experience with everyday urban life. The current programming combines national and international cinema, retrospectives, thematic showcases, restorations, and academic activities. Thus, the precinct maintains a dual function: it safeguards the country's film heritage and offers a space to discover new forms of audiovisual creation in an environment that reflects the cultural vitality of the city.

Did you know...?
The current headquarters took shape after the fire of 1982, which drove the creation of new vaults and specialized laboratories. There are three different venues: Xoco, CENART and Chapultepec.

CINETEC
QUE EL CINE ILUMINE
TU 2026

123

Museo Casa León Trotsky

Address
Av. Río Churubusco 410,
Col. Del Carmen
Metro
Station Coyoacán, Line 3
Station Eje Central, Line 12
Ecobici
CE-655
Hours
Tue-Sun 10:00 - 17:00 h
Entry
Paid admission

Did you know...?
Leon Trotsky was assassinated in this house on August 20, 1940, by Ramón Mercader, Stalin's agent, who attacked him with an ice axe in his study.

In the quiet streets of Coyoacán lies the Museo Casa León Trotsky, a space that preserves intact the memory of one of the most significant political exiles of the twentieth century. Following his expulsion from the Soviet Union, Trotsky and his wife Natalia Sedova settled here in 1939, under strict security measures. Upon crossing its discreet entrance, one perceives not only the daily intimacy of the revolutionary but also the echoes of a history marked by ideology, persecution, and resistance. The house maintains the original furniture, personal objects, and documents that testify to the final years of the Russian revolutionary. In 1940, an armed group burst into the place in a failed assassination attempt, the traces of which can still be observed on the walls. A few months later, Trotsky would finally be attacked in his own study. The garden, surrounded by cacti and flowers, offers a serene contrast to the historical tension of the complex. Under a simple headstone with the hammer and sickle rest the remains of the leader, whose political legacy continues to be a subject of debate and reflection.

124

Museo Nacional de las Intervenciones

Address
20 de Agosto s/n,
Col. San Diego Churubusco
Metro
Station Eje Central, Line 12
Ecobici
CE-650
Hours
Tue-Sun 10:00 - 18:00 h
Entry
Paid admission, free on Sundays

Did you know...?
Every March 17, Saint Patrick's Day, the Mexican government holds an official ceremony in honor of the Saint Patrick's Battalion in the museum's garden.

Located in the neighborhood of San Diego Churubusco, the Museo Nacional de las Intervenciones occupies the former Convento de Nuestra Señora de los Ángeles, founded by Dieguino friars in the seventeenth century. This solid construction of gray quarry stone and sober cloisters was the scene of the Battle of Churubusco on August 20, 1847, during the U.S. intervention. In this place, Mexican forces under the command of General Pedro María Anaya resisted until they exhausted their ammunition, giving rise to the famous phrase: "If there were ammunition, you would not be here." The members of the Saint Patrick's Battalion, Irish immigrants who joined the Mexican army out of religious and ethical conviction, also participated. Inaugurated as a museum in 1981, the precinct addresses the various foreign interventions suffered by Mexico between the nineteenth and twentieth centuries. Its halls exhibit documents, uniforms, paintings, maps, weapons, and engravings that represent the resistance, nationalism, and dignity of the Mexican people.

125

Museo Frida Kahlo

Address
Londres 247, Col. Del Carmen
Metro
Station Viveros and Derechos Humanos, Line 3
Ecobici
CE-658, CE-693
Hours
Tue 10:00 - 18:00 h
Wed 11:00 - 18:00 h
Thu-Sun 10:00 - 18:00 h
Entry
Paid admission

Better known as the Casa Azul, this is one of the most visited cultural spaces in Mexico and a reference for modern art. In this house, Frida Kahlo was born, lived much of her life, and passed away. In 1955, Diego Rivera donated the property to the nation, and a few years later it became a museum. The first museography was designed by the poet Carlos Pellicer, who organized the spaces to preserve the domestic character of the building and show the daily life of the artist. The museum exhibits several of Frida Kahlo's most representative works, along with personal objects, furniture, photographs, and documents that allow insight into her intimate environment. The main spaces—the kitchen, the study, and the garden—maintain their original distribution and reflect her interest in Mexican popular culture and artisanal traditions. The Museo Frida Kahlo is today a cultural symbol of Coyoacán. Every year it receives hundreds of thousands of visitors seeking to know the artistic and personal legacy of one of the most recognized figures of the twentieth century.

Did you know...?
The cobalt blue color of the facade was chosen as a homage to Mexican indigenous tradition. In Mesoamerican cultures, it symbolized water and the sky, elements associated with life and the sacred. Frida Kahlo and Diego Rivera decorated the house with pre-Hispanic pieces, ceramics, and idols that transformed the space into a tangible representation of their Mexican identity and cultural stance regarding European influence.

Frida y Diego
vivieron en
esta casa
1929-1954

126

Mercado de Coyoacán

Address
Ignacio Allende 90,
Col. Del Carmen
Ecobici
CE-695
Hours
Mon-Sun 7:00 - 18:00 h

Did you know...?
The famous *tostadas* of Coyoacán have achieved international renown and appear in gastronomic guides, consolidating the market as a culinary reference in the south of the city.

This market is one of the most representative spaces in the south of Mexico City. It has 400 stalls and is one of the 15 markets designed by Pedro Ramírez Vázquez and Félix Candela. Beyond its proximity to the Museo Frida Kahlo, the market functions as a community hub where neighbors, merchants, and visitors transit among intense colors, fresh aromas, and ingredients that arrive every morning. Eating here is an essential part of the experience: the *fondas* (small eateries) and economic kitchens—many run by families descended from the first stallholders of 1956—offer homemade dishes that have generated loyal clienteles. The market reflects the authentic Coyoacán: diverse, close, and deeply rooted in the memory of the neighborhood. Each aisle shows the continuity of a trade that has known how to adapt without losing its community character.

127

Parroquia de San Juan Bautista

Address
Centenario 8,
Col. Villa Coyoacán
Ecobici
CE-697
Hours
Mon-Sun 7:30 - 19:30 h

Did you know...?
The sacristy preserves an anonymous seventeenth-century painting representing a Franciscan friar levitating during a mystical vision, the origin of an ancient local legend.

With a Baroque facade in dark quarry stone and whitewashed walls, the Iglesia de San Juan Bautista is one of the oldest temples in the Valley of Mexico. It was built over an ancient indigenous ceremonial center and handed over to the Franciscans around 1523, barely two years after the fall of Tenochtitlan. The current Jardín Hidalgo formed part of its atrium, from where the evangelization of the south of the basin was driven. The interior of the temple combines sobriety and monumentality. Its golden altarpiece, the side chapels, and the thick walls testify to an architecture designed to endure, where religion was also an instrument of power. Over the centuries, it has withstood earthquakes, wars, and reforms, remaining one of the main references of Coyoacán's viceregal heritage. Today, it continues to be a meeting point for neighbors and visitors, a space where history, liturgy, and daily life coexist naturally.

128

Plaza y Jardín Hidalgo

Address
Felipe Carrillo Puerto s/n,
Col. Villa Coyoacán
Ecobici
CE-697

Did you know...?
In pre-Hispanic times, this space formed part of the ceremonial center of Coyoacán. During the viceroyalty, it was transformed into a civil nucleus and a place for festivities, processions, and popular markets.

Walking through Plaza Hidalgo means exploring the historic heart of Coyoacán. Surrounded by trees, wrought-iron benches, and old streetlamps, it has been a point of meeting and contemplation for locals and visitors for centuries. The area around it, formed by viceregal mansions of vivid colors, cafés, and bookstores, maintain a bohemian and artistic atmosphere. In the center, the statue of Miguel Hidalgo recalls its role as a civic space and national symbol. Since the viceregal era, the plaza has been the scene of religious celebrations, fairs, and cultural activities that still preserve its community character today. Despite the constant movement, it retains a particular serenity that reflects the identity of Coyoacán: a balance between tradition, daily life, and urban memory.

129

Jardín Centenario

Address
Parque Centenario s/n,
Col. Del Carmen
Ecobici
CE-697

Did you know...?
Under the Jardín Centenario remain viceregal channels that connected Coyoacán with Xochimilco and San Ángel, evidence of the lacustrine past of the valley.

The Jardín Centenario constitutes the symbolic heart of Coyoacán. It was inaugurated in 1910, during the government of Porfirio Díaz, on the occasion of the centennial of the Independence of Mexico, along with the kiosk of the neighboring Plaza Hidalgo. Both spaces formed part of the ancient atrium of the Dominican convent of San Juan Bautista. Although its current layout corresponds to the early twentieth century, the site functioned from the viceregal era as a meeting point for merchants and neighbors, the axis of social life in the town. In its center stands the fountain of the coyotes, a speaking symbol of Coyoacán, surrounded by iron benches and centennial trees that preserve the peaceful character of the place. Opposite the garden rises the so-called House of Hernán Cortés, built in 1755 over a previous construction linked to the early stage of the viceroyalty. Around it, Plaza Hidalgo completes the most representative historical complex of Coyoacán

130

Viveros de Coyoacán

Address
Viveros de Coyoacán, Col. Del Carmen
Metro
Viveros and Derechos Humanos Station, Line 3
Metrobús
Altavista Station, Line 1
Ecobici
CE-659, CE-661, CE-689, CE-663
Hours
Mon-Sun 6:00 - 18:00 h

Did you know...?
The Viveros de Coyoacán were the first urban forestry center in the country. Their model inspired the creation of nurseries and reforestation programs in other Mexican cities during the twentieth century.

The Viveros de Coyoacán are a public green space dedicated to the production of trees and plants for reforestation, administered by the National Forestry Commission (CONAFOR). Located north of the center of Coyoacán, they fulfill a double function: to be a forest nursery and a recreational area for the citizenry. The precinct features delimited paths, rest zones, information modules, and environmental education spaces. It is frequented by people who practice walking or jogging, as it offers a natural environment uncommon within the city. Access with pets is restricted, except in the case of guide dogs. Inside, there are selling points for plants, mainly native species and trees suitable for urban or rural reforestation. Sales are attended by authorized personnel and vary according to the season. More than an urban park, the Viveros de Coyoacán are an environmental laboratory that fosters ecological awareness in the middle of the city.

131

Plaza de Santa Catarina

Address
Jardín Sta. Catarina 10, Col. Santa Catarina
Metro
Viveros and Derechos Humanos Station, Line 3
Ecobici
CE-689, CE-692

Did you know...?
The Dominicans, who arrived in New Spain in 1526, promoted indigenous evangelization through the use of native languages and founded temples and colleges that are still preserved in the south of the country.

The Plaza de Santa Catarina is one of the most peaceful spaces in the historic center of Coyoacán. Smaller in scale than other plazas in the neighborhood, it preserves a quiet and neighborly atmosphere, ideal for those seeking a quiet environment. Surrounded by houses of viceregal architecture and by the parish of Santa Catarina, built in volcanic stone, the plaza maintains its original layout. Inside, there are planters, benches, and a central fountain, without the presence of formal commerce, although the surroundings house coffee shops, workshops, and galleries. The complex owes its name to the Dominican chapel of Santa Catarina de Siena, erected in the sixteenth century as part of an indigenous doctrine. Over time, the place has preserved its residential and pedestrian character, keeping itself apart from mass tourism and conserving the original scale of ancient Coyoacán.

132

Centro Cultural Elena Garro

Address
Fernández Leal 43,
Col. La Concepción
Ecobici
CE-702
Hours
Mon-Sun 10:00 - 21:00 h

Did you know...?
The center bears the name of Elena Garro, one of the most relevant literary figures of the twentieth century in Mexico.

Installed in an early twentieth-century mansion in Coyoacán, this cultural center transforms an ancient residential property into a contemporary space dedicated to reading and community life. The project, developed by architects Fernanda Canales and Saidee Springall, began with a precise intervention that preserved the original structure, the trees of the garden, and the complex's historical proportion. Glass and concrete volumes were added, introducing transparency, natural light, and a direct relationship with the street. The modern facade, conceived as a showcase open to the avenue, allows shelves full of books to be seen from the outside, integrating reading into daily life. Inside, patios, skylights, and existing vegetation organize the routes and generate a serene atmosphere where architecture and nature coexist harmoniously. The program includes a bookstore, halls, classrooms, an exterior forum, and a cafeteria that have made it an active cultural nucleus of Coyoacán.

133

Plaza y Capilla de la Conchita

Address
Fernández Leal 74,
Col. La Concepción
Ecobici
CE-702

Did you know...?
Local tradition states that Hernán Cortés attended private masses in this chapel, built next to his residence while viceregal power was being established in the capital.

In the old neighborhood of San Lucas, in Coyoacán, the Plaza y Capilla de la Conchita is one of the oldest viceregal complexes in Mexico City. Ordered to be built around 1525 by Hernán Cortés, it is considered one of the first Christian temples in America, possibly erected over an ancient indigenous ceremonial center. With a simple layout, the chapel presents a pink quarry stone facade with a Renaissance portal, Doric pilasters, and an image of the Virgin Mary, which gives rise to its dedication. Inside, a sober Baroque altar and a barrel vault with lunettes are preserved. The wooded plaza that surrounds it maintains a viceregal layout and an atmosphere of serenity. Restored by the Instituto Nacional de Antropología e Historia (INAH) in the twentieth century, it forms part of the zone of historical monuments of Coyoacán and stands out as one of its oldest and quietest corners.

134

Fonoteca Nacional

Address
Av. Francisco Sosa 383,
Col. Santa Catarina
Metro
Viveros and Derechos Humanos Station and Miguel Ángel de Quevedo Station, Line 3
Metrobús
La Bombilla Station, Line 1
Ecobici
CE-687
Hours
Mon-Fri 9:00 - 19:00 h
Sat 9:00 - 18:00 h

Did you know...?
The Archivo Fonográfico preserves voices from Mexico's Golden Age of cinema; many artists in the 1940s carried out tests and made historically significant sound recordings there.

In the heart of Coyoacán, at the end of Francisco Sosa Street, the Fonoteca Nacional safeguards the sonic heritage of Mexico. Its headquarters, the Casa de Alvarado, is a seventeenth-century Baroque mansion that owes its name to an ancient—though apocryphal—tradition linking it to Pedro de Alvarado. Declared a Historical Monument in 1935, it retains its viceregal layout and a notable quarry stone portal. Inaugurated in 2008, the Fonoteca preserves more than 600,000 sound records: popular music, historical speeches, soundscapes, old radio, and recordings in indigenous languages. Among its spaces, the Murray Schafer Room, the Sound Art Gallery, and the Octavio Paz Room—who inhabited the house in the thirties—stand out. The property integrates avant-garde technology with a heritage environment. Its archive can be consulted online or at listening stations, reaffirming its role as the guardian of the sound of Mexico.

135

Museo Nacional de la Acuarela Alfredo Guati Rojo

Address
Salvador Novo 88,
Col. Barrio de Santa Catarina
Metro
Miguel Ángel de Quevedo Station, Line 3
Metrobús
La Bombilla Station, Line 1
Ecobici
CE-687, CE-688
Hours
Tue-Sun 10:00 - 18:00 h
Entry
Free admission

Did you know...?
Alfredo Guati Rojo donated his house and personal collection to fund the museum, today run by an independent patronage with international recognition.

In the heart of Coyoacán, the Museo Nacional de la Acuarela "Alfredo Guati Rojo" pays homage to one of the most subtle and complex techniques of painting. Founded in 1967 by master Alfredo Guati Rojo Cárdenas, it was the first museum in Mexico dedicated exclusively to the art of watercolor, and it stands as an international reference for its study and promotion. The museum occupies a restored nineteenth-century mansion with a garden, where more than a thousand works by Mexican and foreign authors are exhibited. Its thematic halls —landscape, portrait, human figure, still life, and abstraction— make possible an appreciation of the versatility of this technique. Furthermore, it organizes temporary exhibitions, workshops, contests, and the International Watercolor Biennial. Recognized by the Instituto Nacional de Bellas Artes y Literatura, the museum continues to disseminate the legacy of its founder and strengthen the presence of watercolor in the Mexican artistic panorama.

136

Museo Nacional de las Culturas Populares

Did you know...?
Unlike other national museums, this venue does not possess a permanent collection: all its exhibitions change constantly to reflect the cultural vitality of Mexico.

Address
Av. Hidalgo 289,
Col. Del Carmen
Metro
General Anaya Station, Line 2
Coyoacán Station, Line 3
Ecobici
CE-700
Hours
Tue-Thu 11:00 - 18:00 h
Fri-Sun 11:00 - 19:00 h
Entry
Paid admission, free on Sundays

Founded in 1982 by anthropologist Guillermo Bonfil Batalla, the Museo Nacional de las Culturas Populares is a space dedicated to the cultural diversity of Mexico. Located in Coyoacán, it promotes the recognition and preservation of the country's living traditions through temporary exhibitions, workshops, film cycles, concerts, and craft fairs. Its architecture, composed of nineteenth-century buildings articulated around patios, reflects the open and communal character that defines the museum. Unlike museums with permanent collections, it privileges a dynamic museography centered on creation and exchange with artisans, artists, and local communities. Among its spaces, the Chapel, adapted for exhibitions, the Quinta Margarita, and the Anexo Moctezuma, where cultural and educational activities take place, stand out. With more than one million annual visitors, the museum has consolidated itself as a national benchmark in the dissemination and valuation of Mexican popular art.

137

Museo de Arte Carrillo Gil

Address
Av. Revolución 1608, Col. San Ángel
Metro
Miguel Ángel de Quevedo Station, Line 3
Metrobús
Altavista Station, Line 1
Ecobici
CE-683
Hours
Mon-Sun 10:00 - 18:00 h
Entry
Paid admission

Did you know...?
The museum safeguards 45 original lithographs by José Clemente Orozco, many with handwritten notes by the artist, which are exhibited only temporarily for conservation reasons.

Opposite the historic neighborhood of San Ángel, the Museo de Arte Carrillo Gil is one of the most relevant museums dedicated to modern and contemporary art in Mexico. Founded in 1974, it was born thanks to the donation of Dr. Álvar Carrillo Gil and his wife Carmen Tejero, who bequeathed one of the most remarkable private collections in the country. The initial collection gathers more than 1,700 works, with pieces by José Clemente Orozco, Diego Rivera, and David Alfaro Siqueiros, as well as artists such as Gunther Gerzso, Wolfgang Paalen, and Luis Nishizawa. Since its opening, the museum has stood out for its experimental spirit, promoting dialogue between its historical collection and contemporary creation. Its functionalist architecture, projected by Fernando Gamboa, houses exhibition halls, a library, workshops, and a specialized documentation center. It is part of the Instituto Nacional de Bellas Artes y Literatura (INBAL) museums' network.

138

Museo Casa Estudio Diego Rivera y Frida Kahlo

Address
Av. Altavista 161,
Col. San Ángel Inn
Hours
Tue-Sun 10:00 - 17:30 h
Entry
Paid admission, free on Sundays

Did you know...?
Diego Rivera's house studio was the first functionalist building in Mexico. Years later, Le Corbusier personally praised O'Gorman, recognizing him as a pioneer of Latin American modernity.

Located on a quiet street in San Ángel, the Museo Casa Estudio Diego Rivera y Frida Kahlo is one of the most significant architectural works of the twentieth century in Mexico. Projected in 1931 by Juan O'Gorman, then just 26 years old, the complex represents the beginning of functionalism in Latin America and a rupture with viceregal and Porfirian tradition. The complex is formed by three volumes: Diego's house, Frida's house, and Cecil O'Gorman's studio. The structures, elevated on pilotis and with flat terraces, respond to a rationalist and austere logic that harmonizes with the environment of the Pedregal. Beyond its form, it was an intimate and creative space: Rivera painted his murals here and Frida found moments of introspection. The bridge that joins both houses symbolizes the intense and complementary relationship of the artists.
The museum preserves furniture, personal objects, and original sketches, offering a direct testimony of Mexican artistic modernity.

139

Plaza e Iglesia de San Jacinto

Address
Madero 2,
Col. San Ángel
Metrobús
La Bombilla Station, Line 1
Ecobici
CE-685

Did you know...?
The chapel of San Jacinto preserves a seventeenth-century altarpiece, one of the oldest in the south of the city, which survived intact the religious expropriations of the nineteenth century.

The Plaza de San Jacinto is one of the most representative spaces of ancient San Ángel and a living testimony of viceregal urbanism in the south of the city. Its origin dates back to the seventeenth century, when the Dominicans built a small chapel and convent surrounded by orchards and country houses. The volcanic and quarry stone facade of the Church refers to the time when San Ángel was a rural settlement, distant from the viceregal bustle. During the viceregal period, the plaza was a meeting point for farmers, travelers, and merchants from neighboring towns. Despite urban transformations, it preserves its intimate layout, flanked by viceregal mansions and cobblestone streets that evoke the rural life of the ancient valley. Inside, sober altarpieces and a garden patio inviting contemplation stand out. Since the mid-twentieth century, the traditional art bazaar has kept the cultural and community vocation of San Ángel alive.

140

Museo de El Carmen

Address
Av. Revolución 4 and 6,
Col. San Ángel
Metrobús
La Bombilla Station, Line 1
Ecobici
CE-685
Hours
Wed-Fri 11:00 - 15:00 h
Sat-Sun 10:00 - 15:00 h
Entry
Paid admission, free on Sundays

Did you know...?
In the crypts of the old convent, twelve naturally mummified bodies were found, preserved by the subsoil conditions. Today they form part of one of the most enigmatic exhibitions of the museum.

Located in the old neighborhood of San Ángel, the Ex Convento y Museo de El Carmen is an essential reference for understanding the religious and artistic life of viceregal Mexico. Founded by the Discalced Carmelites between 1615 and 1628, it was established in a valley south of the city, surrounded by orchards and canals, ideal for spiritual contemplation. The complex, built in sober pink and gray quarry stone and organized around silent patios and cloisters, reflects the austere and mystical character of the order. Over time it functioned as a convent, college, and place of retreat until the exclaustration of the nineteenth century. In 1939 it was transformed into a museum, preserving its original structure and a valuable collection of sacred art. Its collection gathers Novohispanic painting from the seventeenth to the nineteenth centuries—with works by Villalpando, Cabrera, and Alcíbar—as well as sculptures, altarpieces, and liturgical ornaments that evidence the symbolic richness of the Mexican Baroque. To visit it is to reconnect with an era in which art expressed devotion, power, and spirituality.

141

Centro Cultural San Ángel

Address
Av. Revolución s/n,
Col. San Ángel
Metro
Miguel Ángel de Quevedo Station, Line 3
Metrobús
La Bombilla Station, Line 1
Ecobici
CE-685

Did you know...?
The central patio of the Centro Cultural San Ángel preserves a centennial Ahuehuete tree, planted when the building was still a private residence.

Located in the historic heart of San Ángel, the Centro Cultural San Ángel is one of the most representative spaces in the south of Mexico City for artistic and cultural dissemination. The building —an eighteenth-century viceregal mansion—was restored in the 1980s and adapted as a public precinct by the then Departmento del Distrito Federal. With a sober facade and red tile, it preserves masonry walls, interior patios, built-in cupboards, and semicircular arches. It houses galleries, workshops, a library, a scenic forum, and a specialized bookstore. The center organizes exhibitions, book launches, concerts, and film cycles, with a marked community vocation. Throughout the year, the venue actively participates in traditional festivities such as the Feria de las Flores de San Ángel. Its proximity to the Plaza de San Jacinto makes it a mandatory stop for those who tour this ancient town, today a heritage neighborhood of Mexico City.

142

Parque de La Bombilla

Did you know...?
The park takes its name from the La Bombilla restaurant, where on July 17, 1928, Álvaro Obregón was assassinated during a meal celebrated after his presidential re-election.

Address
Av. de la Paz A, Col. Chimalistac
Metro
Miguel Ángel de Quevedo Station, Line 3
Metrobús
La Bombilla Station, Line 1
Ecobici
CE-685

On the border between San Ángel and Chimalistac, the Parque La Bombilla is a reference for modern urbanism in the south of Mexico City. Inaugurated in 1935, during the government of Lázaro Cárdenas, it commemorates the figure of Álvaro Obregón, president of Mexico between 1920 and 1924. The park's layout is organized around an *art déco* monument designed by sculptor Ignacio Asúnsolo, erected on the site where the La Bombilla restaurant was previously located.

The monumental composition, with columns, reliefs, and a central statue of Obregón, originally housed his remains, which were removed in 1989. Despite this, the complex retains its symbolic character and historical burden, evoking the post-revolutionary period and the construction of the modern State. Today, the park is a space for everyday life. Its paths, gardens, and sculptures merge memory and urban life, where history is integrated into the landscape.

143

Parroquia de San Sebastián Mártir

Did you know...?
During the nineteenth century, intellectuals such as Justo Sierra and Manuel Gutiérrez Nájera walked through the streets of Chimalistac in search of inspiration.

144

Barrio y Puentes de Chimalistac

Address
Federico Gamboa 11, Col. Chimalistac
Metro
Miguel Ángel de Quevedo Station, Line 3
Metrobús
La Bombilla Station and Doctor Gálvez Station, Line 1
Ecobici
CE-661, CE-85
Hours
Thu-Tue 7:00 - 19:00 h

Chimalistac preserves one of the best-preserved viceregal scenes in the city: cobblestone streets, narrow alleys, small plazas, and stone bridges that follow the historical course of the Magdalena River. Its layout combines a pre-Hispanic past with the imprint of the Carmelites of San Ángel, who defined much of its physiognomy through a hydraulic system that irrigated orchards and connected the different sectors of the town. Among the most distinctive elements are the bridges, the Puente del Púlpito, the Puente del Carmen, and the Puente de Oxtopulco, each accesible from the Paseo del Río, where nature and memory intertwine. The Parroquia de San Sebastián Mártir stands in the heart of neighborhood, built toward the end of the seventeenth century on Carmelite lands. Its sober architecture made of volcanic stone walls reflects an introspective character that is reinforced by the light filtering through the trees. The atrium, with its quarry stone cross and lichen-covered walls, maintains the historical configuration of this ancient religious center, which continues to function as a landmark for the community.

145

Ciudad Universitaria
UNAM

Address
Col. Ciudad Universitaria
Metro
Universidad Station and Copilco Station, Line 3
Metrobús
Cd. Universitaria Station and Centro Cultural Universitario Station, Line 1

The central campus of the Universidad Nacional Autónoma de México (UNAM), is one of the most emblematic architectural, artistic, and urban projects of the twentieth century in Latin America. Inaugurated in 1954, its construction transformed the landscape of the volcanic bedrock of the south of the city into a monumental complex that integrates modernist architecture, mural art, and the natural environment. The design was a collective work of architects such as Mario Pani, Enrique del Moral, José Villagrán García, Pedro Ramírez Vázquez, Carlos Lazo, and Félix Candela, among others. The volcanic stone of the site was reused in walls and plazas, integrating the campus into the landscape.

In 2007, UNESCO inscribed the central campus on the World Heritage List, recognizing it as "a monumental collective work of twentieth-century modernism." The complex is organized around "Las Islas," a central green space that articulates iconic buildings such as the Biblioteca Central, the Rectory Tower, and the Estadio Olímpico Universitario. In addition to its academic function, Ciudad Universitaria is a cultural and scientific center of national scope: it houses museums, libraries, the Sala Nezahualcóyotl, and the Centro Cultural Universitario. Scenario of the 1968 Olympic Games and historical student movements, its layout remains a symbol of the public spirit, critical thought, and university identity of Mexico.

Did you know...?
Ciudad Universitaria brings together more than 110 murals that express the synthesis between art, science, and education. Among the most emblematic are the Biblioteca Central by Juan O'Gorman; the Torre de Rectoría, where David Alfaro Siqueiros depicted *Las fechas en la historia de México o el derecho a la cultura*; and the Estadio Olímpico Universitario, with reliefs by Diego Rivera. Together with the works of José Chávez Morado and Francisco Eppens, these murals turned UNAM into the epicenter of modern public art in Mexico.

146

Biblioteca Central
UNAM

Address
Circuito Interior s/n,
Ciudad Universitaria
Metro
Copilco Station, Line 3
Metrobús
Doctor Gálvez Station, Line 1
Hours
Mon-Sun 8:30 - 21:30 h

Did you know...?
The mural was planned to be read continuously when walking around the building: its narrative does not begin or end on a single facade but functions as a symbolic cycle without a fixed entry point.

This library, inaugurated in 1956, is one of the most representative architectural and cultural symbols of the UNAM. The project, developed by Juan O'Gorman together with Gustavo María Saavedra and Juan Martínez de Velasco, started from the idea of integrating art, architecture, and function into a single organism. Its facade is covered by a monumental mosaic made with natural stones from different regions of the country, whose tones—more than 150—guarantee the permanence of color and give the building a solid and enduring presence. The mural, titled *Representación histórica de la cultura*, is one of the largest mosaics in the world and organizes its four facades as a great stone codex. Each wall alludes to a distinct period of the history of Mexico through a symbolic language inspired by Mesoamerican worldviews and dualities that articulate past and present.
The collection exceeds 1,400,000 volumes and includes the Fondo Antiguo with copies from the fifteenth to the eighteenth centuries, making it a fundamental reference for academic life of Mexico.

147

Estadio Olímpico Universitario

Address
Av. Insurgentes s/n, Ciudad Universitaria
Metro
Copilco Station, Line 3
Metrobús
Doctor Gálvez Station, Line 1

Did you know...?
Its construction was carried out in an exceptionally short period—around eight months—making it one of the most ambitious projects of modern Mexican architecture.

Inaugurated in 1952, this precinct was the first major construction of Ciudad Universitaria and one of the founding elements of the architectural complex of UNAM. The project, developed by Augusto Pérez Palacios, Jorge Bravo, and Raúl Salinas Moro, was integrated into the landscape of the Pedregal de San Ángel through the extensive use of volcanic stone, which visually links it with the environment and the characteristic geology of the zone. Its asymmetrical form breaks with the traditional typology of stadiums and favors spatial continuity with neighboring buildings. The eastern facade features Diego Rivera's relief mural *La Universidad, la familia y el deporte en México*, executed with colored stones and composed of pre-Hispanic, university, and modern symbols. Rivera conceived this work as part of a broader mural program that he could not conclude. The stadium hosted the ceremonies and Olympic competitions of 1968 and today continues to be a symbol of university identity and a fundamental precinct for the sporting and social life of UNAM.

148

Centro Cultural Universitario
CCU

Address
Av. Insurgentes Sur 3000, Ciudad Universitaria
Metro
Universidad Station, Line 3
Metrobús
Centro Cultural Universitario Station, Line 1

UNAM's Centro Cultural Universitario is one of the most extensive and relevant cultural complexes in Latin America. Built between 1976 and 1980, it concentrates spaces dedicated to contemporary art, music, cinema, theater, and research, becoming a key point for understanding university cultural life. Its scale and diversity make it a fundamental destination for comprehending the role of the institution in the Mexican artistic tradition. Contemporary art finds a central reference in the Museo Universitario de Arte Contemporáneo (MUAC), designed by Teodoro González de León, while cinematographic activity has a continuous presence in the José Revueltas and Julio Bracho screening rooms. The Carlos Chávez Hall and the Miguel Covarrubias Hall are key stages for concerts, dance, and scenic spectacles. Theater occupies a prominent place within the Juan Ruiz de Alarcón Theater, the Sor Juana Inés de la Cruz Forum, and the University Theater Center, where generations of artists have been trained. Next to them is one of the most recognized acoustic precincts on the continent: the Sala Nezahualcóyotl, home of the UNAM Philharmonic Orchestra and famous for its acoustics. At the southern end of the complex, the Espacio Escultórico, a monumental circle of sculptures arranged on the petrified lava of the Xitle volcano, represents one of the most singular works of contemporary Mexican art. The CCU also includes the Biblioteca Nacional y Hemeroteca, as well as research centers dedicated to the production and study of university knowledge.

Did you know...?
The Sala Nezahualcóyotl was the first in Mexico designed with a vineyard-style, which allows for a homogeneous sound experience from any point in the venue.

149

Ruta de la Amistad

Address
Periférico
Blvd. Adolfo Ruiz Cortines,
Col. Insurgentes Cuicuilco
Metrobús
Perisur Station, Line 1

Did you know...?
Several sculptures of the Ruta de la Amistad were conceived to align with the path of the sun and the shadows projected on the volcanic lava, which caused their perception to change radically depending on the time of day and the direction of traffic.

Created for the 1968 Olympic Games as part of the Cultural Olympiad, this sculptural corridor brought together nineteen monumental pieces installed along approximately 17 km in the south of Mexico City. The works, made by prominent artists from different countries, were conceived as a gesture of international fraternity and as a permanent legacy for the city. Built primarily in pigmented concrete, they were integrated into the landscape, then characterized by extensive surfaces of lava from the ancient Xitle and by agricultural zones linked to Xochimilco. The project, devised by Mathias Goeritz in dialogue with architect Pedro Ramírez Vázquez, started from the idea that art should function as a symbol of union between nations. The sculptures were designed to be seen from the roadway and to dialogue with the territory: some emerge directly from the volcanic stone, while others open toward the environment as abstract structures that accompany the movement of traffic. Each work responds to the aesthetic language of its author, without narrative intention, but with the objective of offering a continuous and accessible visual journey for anyone passing through the zone. Urban growth drastically changed the original context. Several pieces were hidden, deteriorated, or surrounded by environments very different from those foreseen. For years, the corridor remained relatively abandoned, until the 1990s, when rescue efforts, driven by specialists and citizens interested in recovering the coherence of the complex began. Some sculptures remained in place; others were moved to save them from road works or to restore the sequence proposed for 1968. Today the Ruta de la Amistad is recognized as cultural heritage of the city.

1. *Señales*, Ángela Gurría (Mexico)
2. *El ancla*, Willy Guttman (Switzerland)
3. *Las Tres Gracias*, Miloslav Chlupac (Czechoslovakia)
4. *Sol*, Kyoshi Takahashi (Japan)
5. *El sol bípedo*, Pierre Székely (Hungary)
6. *La Torre de los Vientos*, Gonzalo Fonseca (Uruguay)
7. *Hombre de Paz*, Constantino Nivola (Italy)
8. *Disco solar*, Jacques Moeschal, (Belgium)
9. *Sin título*, Todd Williams (United States of America)
10. *Reloj solar*, Grzegorz Kowalski (Poland)
11. *Monumento a las Olimpiadas de México*, Josep Maria Subirachs (Spain)
12. *Janus*, Clement Meadmore (Australia)
13. *Muro articulado*, Herbert Bayer (Austria-United States of America)
14. *Tertulia de gigantes*, Joop J. Beljon (Netherlands)
15. *Puerta de Paz*, Itzhak Danziger (Israel)
16. *Sin título*, Olivier Seguin (France)
17. *Charamusca Africana*, Mohamed Melehi (Morocco)
18. *Sin título*, Jorge Dubon (Mexico)
19. *Puerta al viento*, Helen Escobedo (Mexico)

Guests

1. *El sol rojo*, Alexander Calder (United States of America)
2. *La Osa Mayor*, Mathias Goeritz (Mexico)
3. *Hombre corriendo*, Germán Cueto (Mexico)

150

Museo Anahuacalli

Address
Museo 150,
Col. San Pablo Tepetlapa
Tren Ligero
Nezahualpilli Station
Hours
Tue-Sun 11:00 - 18:00 h
Entry
Paid admission

Conceived by Diego Rivera and built with volcanic stone from the Pedregal, this museum is one of the most singular architectural works of the twentieth century in Mexico. The project began in 1946, when Rivera invited architect Juan O'Gorman to collaborate on the creation of a building that would function as a container for his collection of pre-Hispanic art. Although the painter did not live to see it concluded—he died in 1957—the work was finalized by O'Gorman, Ruth Rivera Marín, and Heriberto Pagelson. The building, built with basalt extracted from the area, combines a modern structure with pre-Hispanic inspiration. Its battered walls, serpentine pilasters, and rhomboidal doors refer to Toltec and Maya architecture, while its quadrangular plan and symbolic disposition evoke Mesoamerican temples. The result is a monumental and introspective space where art, architecture, and worldview dialogue in profound unity.
The museum houses more than 2,000 archaeological pieces from different Mesoamerican cultures, acquired by Rivera. From the Preclassic period, the female figurines of Tlatilco stand out, along with many other pieces representative of diverse Mesoamerican cultures, sculptures dedicated to Ehécatl-Quetzalcóatl, and representations of warriors of the highest rank within Mexica society. In Rivera's own study, sketches, work tools, and early works are preserved, revealing the influence of pre-Hispanic art on his mural painting.

Did you know...?
In 2021, Taller Mauricio Rocha completed the expansion, which includes the reuse of existing structures, three buildings for offices, workshops and storage, and new public spaces.

151

Zona Arqueológica de Cuicuilco

Address
Av. Insurgentes Sur s/n,
Col. Insurgentes Cuicuilco
Metrobús
Villa Olímpica Station,
Line 1
Hours
Tue-Sun 9:00 - 17:00 h
Entry
Free admission

Did you know...?
Beneath the lava, the INAH continues to uncover intact remains of pre-Hispanic dwellings and utensils, as Cuicuilco was the first recorded center of civilization in the Basin of Mexico.

The Pyramid of Cuicuilco is one of the oldest vestiges of the central highlands. Its construction began around 700 BC and reached its apogee between 400 BC and 100 AD, centuries before Teotihuacan. Considered the first great urban ceremonial center of the valley, it stands out for its circular structure of volcanic stone and clay, 17 m high and more than 100 m in diameter. At its summit, ceremonies linked to the solar and agricultural calendar were performed. Around the year 250 AD, the eruption of the Xitle volcano buried the city under lava, causing its abandonment and the migration of its population toward other regions. Rediscovered at the end of the nineteenth century, it was excavated in the twentieth by Byron Cummings and Manuel Gamio. Today, a part of the site is preserved as a protected archaeological zone in the middle of the urban landscape.

152

Pilares Cuicuilco

Address
Zapote 159,
Col. Zapote I, II and III
Metrobús
Villa Olímpica Station,
Line 1

Did you know...?
Its inverted roof not only captures rainwater: it also helps regulate the interior temperature, making a shared use of the space more comfortable throughout the year.

Mexico City's PILARES—Points of Innovation, Freedom, Art, Education and Knowledge—are spaces proposed by the city government to host cultural activities suited to the demographics, needs and interests of the population in the area they are located. PILARES Cuicuilco is the first of three projects emerging from the collaboration between TO, +UdeB and AGENdA. It is a response to two main concerns: water management, resolved with a pitched roof designed to collect rainwater and act as a buffer for periods of water scarcity in the city; and replicability, resolved by means of a structure comprising lightweight metal and timber elements to facilitate construction, giving priority to flexibility of spaces in the event of a change of use. Furthermore, the materials used in the façade suggest a permeable skin, providing easy access and connecting the building with the city.

153

Centro de Tlalpan

Address
Plaza de la Constitución s/n, Col. Tlalpan Centro
Metrobús
Fuentes Brotantes Station, Line 1

Did you know...?
Tlalpan means "place on firm land" in Nahuatl. It was once called San Agustín de las Cuevas, and the first telephone call in Mexico City was made from here.

South of the city, Tlalpan's historic center combines tradition, culture, and daily life among cobblestone streets and viceregal mansions that preserve their historical character, with a vitality expressed in its gastronomy, its markets, and its cultural activities. Among its main attractions, the Parroquia de San Agustín, built in the sixteenth century, and the Plaza de la Constitución, the heart of the neighborhood and a community meeting point, stand out. The traditional market, along with cafés and galleries, reinforces its commercial and cultural vocation. Of pre-Hispanic origin, Tlalpan was inhabited by Nahua and Matlatzinca groups before the conquest. During the viceregal period, it consolidated itself as a resting point on the route toward Cuernavaca and the south of the country. In the nineteenth century, it maintained its regional relevance and intense agricultural and livestock activity. Integrated into the capital in the twentieth century, the center preserves its viceregal layout and its character as a historical enclave within the contemporary metropolis.

154

Estadio Banorte

Address
Calz. de Tlalpan 3465,
Col. Santa Úrsula Coapa
Tren Ligero
Estadio Azteca Station

Did you know...?
This is the only venue in the world that has hosted three FIFA World Cups: Mexico 1970, Mexico 1986, and the upcoming 2026. This is where the two most celebrated goals in football history were scored: Maradona's "Hand of God" in 1986 and Pelé's goal in the 1970 World Cup final.

This stadium stands south of Mexico City and is a symbol of modern Mexican architecture. Inaugurated on May 29, 1966 and designed by architects Pedro Ramírez Vázquez and Rafael Mijares Alcérreca, it became the most important venue for national soccer and the stage for major international competitions. Its construction, carried out on rugged, igneous terrain, involved complex engineering work that marked a before and after in the country's sports infrastructure. With a capacity for more than 83,000 spectators, it is a space of collective meeting where sport, culture, and spectacle converge. It has been the habitual home of the Mexican national team, as well as the home of Club América and Club Cruz Azul in different periods. Here, league titles, international tournaments, and Copa Libertadores finals have been contested. Beyond soccer, the stadium has hosted concerts by artists such as Michael Jackson, Paul McCartney, U2, Shakira, Coldplay, and Juan Gabriel, in addition to religious and cultural events. As part of the Ruta de la Amistad, sculptor Alexander Calder designed *El sol rojo*, installed outside the stadium.

7

Xochimilco

Xochimilco is one of the oldest and most continuous territories of human settlement in the Basin of Mexico. Its occupation predates the consolidation of the great urban centers of the Postclassic period and developed in close relation to the lacustrine system that, for centuries, shaped the economic, social, and symbolic life of the region. Unlike other areas of the ancient lake, Xochimilco has managed to preserve—despite profound political, urban, and environmental transformations—a significant part of its hydraulic landscape.

It is characterized by its network of canals and *chinampas*, an agricultural system that remains active to this day and constitutes one of the most eloquent testimonies of Mesoamerican engineering. The *chinampas* were not simple cultivation plots, but rather a complex technology based on the precise management of water, the stabilization of lacustrine soil, and the constant generation of fertile land through organic sediments. This model enabled intensive and sustained agricultural production, capable of supplying large populations and integrating into regional exchange networks without disrupting the ecological balance of the environment.

After the conquest, Xochimilco maintained its importance as a productive zone within the new viceregal order. During the viceregal centuries, the chinampa landscape adapted to new forms of property, administration, and taxation, yet it essentially preserved its hydraulic and agricultural logic. This continuity made it a key space for the survival of productive practices of pre-Hispanic origin within the framework of the viceregal economy.

Throughout the nineteenth century, it became one of the valley's main agricultural and lacustrine corridors, even as major drainage projects began to transform the basin irreversibly. In the twentieth century, faced with advancing urbanization and the near-total loss of the ancient lakes, Xochimilco acquired a singular symbolic and heritage value: it came to be recognized as the last living vestige of the pre-Hispanic hydraulic system. The preservation of the *chinampa* zone and its network of canals led to its designation as a UNESCO World Heritage Site in 1987, in recognition of its historical, cultural, and environmental value. Today, Xochimilco is a hybrid and complex territory: at once an ecological reserve, an agricultural space in resistance, and an international tourist destination.

Calzada de las Bombas
Periférico
Calzada del Hueso
Canal de Miramontes
Armada de México
Calzada Acoxpa
Periférico
164
165
PARQUE ECOLÓGICO DE XOCHIMILCO
Muyuguarda
Antiguo Canal Cuemanco
Cam. a La Ciénega
162
Prol. División del Norte
La Noria
155
Mexico
Guadalupe I. Ramírez
AMPLIACIÓN
LA NORIA
Huichapan
161
160
Pino
159
163
BARRIO
EL ROSARIO
SANTA
CRUCITA
156
Francisco Goitia
Xochimilco
Nuevo Leór
Cam. a San Pablo
Acueducto
Redención
Francisco Goytia
BARRIO
BELÉN
CALTONGO
SANTA CRU
ACALPIXCA
157
16 de Septiembre
Tenochtitlan
0
250
500m

Route 7 / Xochimilco

155 Museo Dolores Olmedo
156 Panteón de Xilotepec
157 Mercado de las Flores San Luis Tlaxialtemalco
158 Museo Arqueológico de Xochimilco
159 Mercado de Xochimilco
160 Catedral de San Bernardino de Siena
161 Jardín Juárez
162 Zona Chinampera
163 Embarcadero de Caltongo
164 Pista de Canotaje Virgilio Uribe
165 Parque Ecológico de Xochimilco

155

Museo Dolores Olmedo

Address
Av. México 5843, Col. La Noria
Tren Ligero
La Noria Station
Hours
Tue-Sun 10:00 - 18:00 h
Entry
Paid admission

Did you know...?
The Museo Dolores Olmedo houses the most extensive collection of works by Frida Kahlo, one of the most internationally recognized Mexican artists, along with pieces by Angelina Beloff, Pablo O'Higgins, and pre-Hispanic and viceregal art.

Open to the public on September 17, 1994, in La Noria, this museum is located in a viceregal estate dating from the sixteenth century that over time served both as a residence and a military barracks. The property was adapted to house the collection assembled by Mexican businesswoman and philanthropist Dolores Olmedo, who sought to offer a broad view of Mexican art and culture. The museum safeguards 26 works by Frida Kahlo and 148 by Diego Rivera, as well as pieces of pre-Hispanic, viceregal, and popular art. Convinced of the value of popular art and the cultural construction of Mexican identity, Olmedo conceived a museological project that would integrate the four major stages of the country's cultural history within a single space. For more than fifty years, she also promoted and financed museums such as Casa Azul and Anahuacalli. The museum's layout brings together historic architecture, gardens, and exhibition galleries to present a panorama that allows visitors to understand the multiple layers through which Mexican cultural identity has been conceived.

156

Panteón de Xilotepec

Address
Mártires de Río Blanco and México, Camino a San Pablo, Col. Ampliación la Noria

Tren Ligero
Huichapan Station

Hours
Mon-Sun 8:00 - 15:00 h

Did you know...?
The cemetery chapel retains elements that refer to older devotional structures of the town, a visible testimony to the long religious tradition associated with this funerary space.

The Panteón de Xilotepec is one of the oldest and most representative funerary spaces in Xochimilco. Its location in the highest part of the town allows for an understanding of the relationship between the riverside settlements and the elevated areas destined for community shelter, worship, and, over time, burial.
The cemetery attests the population continuity of Xilotepec through graves that span more than a century and reflect changes in funerary practices, religious iconography, and family organization. Between the late nineteenth century and the early twentieth century, it was consolidated as a formal cemetery, following the tradition of locating these spaces on hills associated with protection and purification. During the twentieth century, it expanded gradually and integrated family burials, common graves, and a chapel that replaced previous structures. Its orderly layout and close link to the life of the town keep it as a setting for processions and commemorations, as well as a reference point for understanding the historical evolution of the town and its position between the *chinampa* zone and the surrounding slopes.

157

Mercado de las Flores San Luis Tlaxialtemalco

Address
Guadalupe I. Ramírez,
Pueblo San Luis Tlaxialtemalco
Hours
Mon-Sun 9:00 - 18:00 h

Did you know...?
This market produces plants for reforestation programs throughout the city and maintains collections of species native to the lacustrine basin including some listed as sensitive due to their ecological importance.

Dedicated to plant production for environmental and urban projects, this plant nursery is one of the most important centers in the south of the city and a key piece in the conservation of the *chinampa* zone and the ecosystems associated with the wetlands. Its work focuses on the reproduction and cultivation of ornamental, forest, and native species used in reforestation, ecological restoration, and green area maintenance programs. The property integrates greenhouses, open-air cultivation areas, irrigation ponds, and storage zones organized technically to guarantee plant quality. Its operation is linked to the agricultural tradition of Xochimilco, where the relationship between water, land, and cultivation has been central for centuries. Established in the mid-twentieth century as part of government initiatives to supply vegetation to the city, it increased its relevance with urban growth and the need to recover degraded areas. Over time, it incorporated native wetland species and cultivation techniques related to *chinampa* knowledge.

158

Museo Arqueológico de Xochimilco

Address
Av. Tenochtitlan s/n,
Col. Santa Cruz Acalpixca
Hours
Tue-Sun 10:00 - 17:00 h
Entry
Paid admission

Did you know...?
The museum's collection includes ceramics spanning more than a thousand years of technical and stylistic development, revealing local variations that do not appear in other traditions south of the valley.

Dedicated to the safeguarding, study, and exhibition of pre-Hispanic heritage found in the lacustrine region of the southern Valley of Mexico, the museum offers a comprehensive view of cultural processes prior to Mexica hegemony and of the social, agricultural, and ritual dynamics of the ancient Xochimilca lordship. Its collection gathers sculptures, utensils, construction materials, and objects associated with agricultural production and ceremonial life, coming from local excavations. Founded in the second half of the twentieth century to concentrate scattered archaeological materials, it emerged in response to the risk faced by findings due to hydraulic works and changes in land use. Since then, it has integrated pieces recovered in neighborhoods, hills, and *chinampa* zones, and has developed permanent and temporary exhibitions that contextualize the regional importance of the Xochimilca lordship before its incorporation into the Mexica sphere. Its museography highlights the relationship between the lacustrine landscape, agricultural engineering, and daily life, and evidences the cultural continuity of the territory.

159

Mercado de Xochimilco

Address
Av. Nuevo León s/n,
Col. Santa Crucita
Tren Ligero
Xochimilco Station
Hours
Mon-Sun 8:00 - 20:00 h

Did you know...?
Many of the producers selling in the market come directly from active *chinampas*, keeping alive the agricultural tradition that distinguishes Xochimilco, especially visible in the seasonal sale of local flowers and medicinal herbs.

With a long tradition linked to regional agricultural exchange, the Mercado de Xochimilco reflects the economic and social continuity that has defined Xochimilco since pre-Hispanic times. Although the current building reflects twentieth-century interventions, it still follows the logic of the ancient lacustrine *tianguis*, where products from *chinampas*, orchards, and riverside communities were distributed. The market commercially articulates the downtown neighborhoods and offers local production: vegetables, flowers, medicinal herbs, seeds, and food prepared with traditional techniques. Daily activities coexist with seasonal practices, such as selling plants for Holy Week or the concentration of flower growers during the Día de Muertos season. Its dynamic maintains a direct link with the *chinampa* system because, historically, Xochimilco *tianguis* were linked to lacustrine routes and, during the twentieth century, their reorganization allowed for the consolidation of a formal market that preserves the agricultural and floricultural tradition of the region.

160

Catedral de San Bernardino de Siena

Address
Av. Nuevo León 22,
Col. Santa Crucita
Tren Ligero
Xochimilco Station
Hours
Mon-Sun 7:00 - 20:00 h

Did you know...?
The recent restoration revealed viceregal pictorial layers hidden beneath later plaster and recovered historical finishes and original elements, exposed once again after stabilizing walls and roofs affected by humidity and ground subsidence.

Recognized as the most important religious complex in Xochimilco, this ancient conventual compound reflects the transition between the first evangelization constructions of the sixteenth century and the expansions that accompanied the consolidation of viceregal dominion. Composed of a temple, atrium, and ancient conventual dependencies, it has functioned since its origin as an urban and ceremonial axis that articulates the community life of the Xochimilca neighborhoods. Its relevance is due as much to its antiquity as to the continuity of its use: for centuries it has been a space for catechesis, a parish center, and a meeting point for festivities, as well as a visual landmark of the urban landscape. In recent years, the Secretaría de Cultura Federal carried out a comprehensive restoration aimed at stabilizing the structure, recovering historical finishes, and safeguarding artistic and documentary pieces, correcting damage caused by humidity, movements of the lacustrine subsoil, and wear derived from continuous use. Today it stands as an architectural and social testimony that synthesizes five centuries of urban transformation in Xochimilco.

161

Jardín Juárez

Address
Jardín Juárez,
Col. Barrio El Rosario
Tren Ligero
Xochimilco Station

Did you know...?
The current layout of the Central Plaza of Xochimilco follows the viceregal model of the plaza mayor, where civil, religious, and commercial functions converged, and whose surroundings housed a *tianguis* that supplied nearby communities.

This is the wooded sector of the grand central plaza of Xochimilco and functions as a transition between the civic space and the neighborhoods. It occupies part of the ancient atrium of the Parroquia de San Bernardino de Siena, whose facade rises at the eastern end of the plaza. Its current layout integrates paths, shaded areas, a central kiosk, and monuments that reflect local public life.
To the south stands the clock tower, visible from different points of the plaza, and further on the Mercado de Xochimilco. Due to its strategic location, Jardín Juárez is a well-known meeting point for visitors and locals heading to the docks or the historic neighborhoods of the center.
It also marks the northern limit of the plaza before the start of Barrio El Rosario. It is a resting space for those crossing the esplanade or returning from the canals, and its blend of shade, pedestrian circulation, and proximity to access points makes it a key node for starting or concluding tours of Xochimilco.

162

Zona Chinampera

Address
Area between Isla de las Muñecas and Embarcadero de Caltongo
Access
Via trajinera tours or defined paths

Did you know...?
The *chinampa* is considered one of the most regenerative and environmentally friendly agricultural systems created by humankind.

The *chinampa* zone of Xochimilco forms part of the traditional lacustrine cultivation system developed in the basin of the ancient Lake Xochimilco, southeast of Mexico City. It consists of *chinampas*: elongated plots built through the accumulation of sediments and plant matter, delimited by navigable canals that allow access by *trajineras*. This ensemble constitutes a productive and cultural ecosystem where intensive agriculture, horticulture, and recreational activities converge. The *chinampa* system emerged among the pre-Hispanic inhabitants of the Basin of Mexico as a response to the lacustrine environment and reached its greatest development with the Mexica. After the conquest, a few modifications were made to its use. During the nineteenth and twentieth centuries, the desiccation of the basin and urban growth significantly reduced the original extent of the system. Faced with this process, starting in the second half of the twentieth century, public policies were promoted for the protection of *chinampa* soil and the lagoon system of Xochimilco, oriented toward conserving this traditional agricultural ecosystem at risk of disappearing. Despite pressures derived from urban expansion, soil fragmentation, and environmental deterioration, the *chinampas* still contribute with fresh food to the city and form a living landscape of high ecological and cultural value. The network of canals, riparian vegetation, and the agricultural structures themselves make up a heritage that requires active management to ensure its conservation and sustainable functioning.

163

Embarcadero de Caltongo

Address
Av. Nuevo León 113,
Col. Caltongo
Hours
Mon-Sun 9:00 - 22:00 h

Did you know...?
From Caltongo, boat routes cross *chinampa* areas that are still productive. Many are operated by boatmen coming from families that have worked in the lacustrine system for generations, preserving traditional navigation practices.

As one of the most relevant accesses to the canal system of Xochimilco, the Embarcadero de Caltongo allows for an understanding of the historical organization of the *chinampa* zone. It articulates contemporary transit —tourist and community-based— with lacustrine routes of pre-Hispanic origin, and offers access to canals that preserve ancient layouts and maintain agricultural activity, reflecting the continuity of a unique productive landscape in the Valley of Mexico. Caltongo functions as a logistical node that concentrates *trajineras*, *chinampa* workers, routes toward conservation areas, and access to tourist circuits. Unlike other docks focused exclusively on tourism, it maintains a balance between local uses and visitor services, becoming a privileged point for observing the social dynamics of the territory. Its proximity to active agricultural zones allows for the appreciation of traditional activities such as the transport of plants and materials. Historically, it was a natural entryway to cultivation areas and, since the twentieth century, it was consolidated as a formal infrastructure that preserves connections with operating *chinampas*.

164

Pista de Canotaje Virgilio Uribe

Address
Periférico Sur s/n,
Col. Cuemanco
Hours
Mon-Fri 8:00 - 19:00 h
Sat-Sun 7:00 - 19:00 h

Did you know...?
Its linear layout responds to the adaptation of a lacustrine landscape that was originally more irregular, and its design followed international specifications for the canoeing and rowing events of 1968, establishing an unprecedented standard in the city.

This emblematic sports facility south of the city constitutes one of the most significant legacies of the 1968 Olympic Games. Built on a strip of the ancient lacustrine system, it regularized and adapted a body of water to allow for canoeing and rowing competitions under international standards, integrating modern infrastructure into an environment where active canals and *chinampas* subsisted.
It articulates high-performance sports, environmental conservation, and community training. It has hosted national and international competitions, training centers, and educational activities, and its permanence highlights the historical relationship between Xochimilco and water, reinterpreted in a contemporary key. The course also serves as an environmental laboratory for water quality monitoring and aquatic ecosystem management. In the urban sphere, it represents an example of the adaptation of sports infrastructure on terrain subject to subsidence and hydrological variations with historical lacustrine dynamics.

165

Parque Ecológico de Xochimilco

Address
Periférico Oriente 1,
Col. Ciénega Grande
Hours
Tue-Sun 9:00 - 17:00 h

Did you know...?
It houses one of the most important scientific sanctuaries for the monitoring of the axolotl, and its artificial lagoons reproduce the hydraulic dynamics of the ancient lakes of the basin, forming part of the polygon protected as World Heritage.

Inaugurated in 1993 as part of a broad environmental rescue project in response to the declaration of Xochimilco as a World Heritage site by UNESCO in 1987, the Parque Ecológico de Xochimilco was conceived to reverse decades of wetland deterioration and recover the historic image of the canals and *chinampas*. Its creation responded to the need to restore the natural environment and ensure propitious conditions for the continuity of the lacustrine ecosystem. Since then, it has received maintenance

interventions and conservation actions destined to guarantee the survival of native species and the stability of the hydraulic system. Today, it is one of the most relevant environmental spaces in the south of Mexico City and one of the few regions where the original lacustrine structure of the valley is still preserved.
The project integrates protected areas, paths, artificial lagoons, and bird-watching zones, making it a key site for understanding the historical relationship between the environment and human life in Xochimilco. Its design, organized around the traditional hydraulic system, explains how bodies of water have modeled the landscape from the pre-Hispanic era to the present. Conceived as a biological corridor, the park favors the permanence of emblematic native species, such as the axolotl, and also functions as an educational space to promote environmental awareness. It offers a unique opportunity for locals and turists to observe up close ecological processes that have defined the identity of Xochimilco and to understand the importance of protecting the aquatic systems that have historically sustained life in the valley.

MOVILIDAD INTEGRADA DE LA CIUDAD DE MÉXICO

UNA CIUDAD, UN SISTEMA

SISTEMA DE TRANSPORTE COLECTIVO METRO

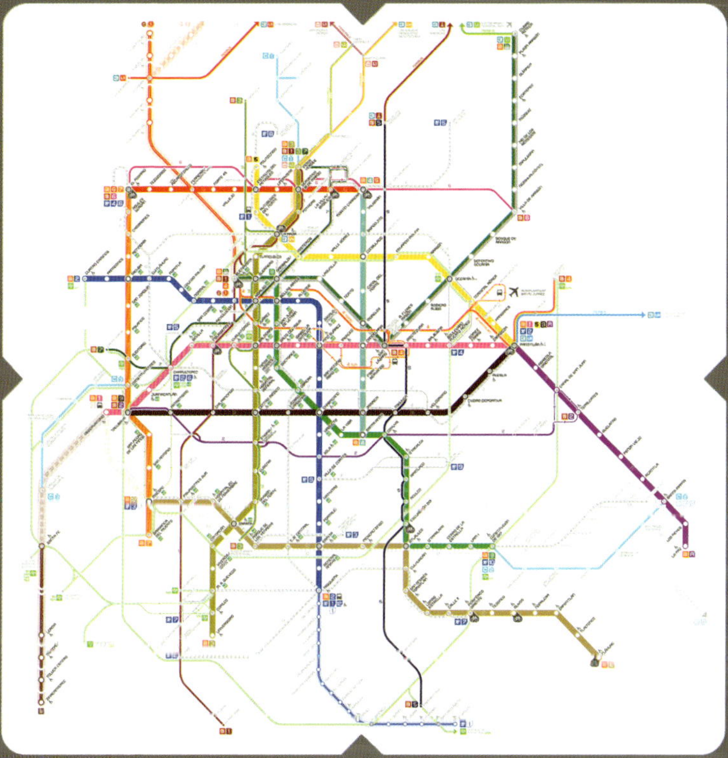

STC METRO
LUNES A VIERNES 05:00-00:00 HORAS
SÁBADOS 05:00-00:00 HORAS
DOMINGOS Y FESTIVOS 05:00-00:00 HORAS

METROBÚS
LUNES A VIERNES 04:30-00:00 HORAS
SÁBADOS 04:30-00:00 HORAS
DOMINGOS Y FESTIVOS 05:00-00:00 HORAS

TREN LIGERO
LUNES A VIERNES 05:00-23:30 HORAS
SÁBADOS 06:00-23:30 HORAS
DOMINGOS Y FESTIVOS 07:00-23:30 HORAS

TROLEBÚS
LUNES A VIERNES 05:00-00:00 HORAS
SÁBADOS 05:00-00:00 HORAS
DOMINGOS Y FESTIVOS 06:00-00:00 HORAS
05:00-00:00 LÍNEA 10

CABLEBÚS
LUNES A VIERNES 05:00-23:00 HORAS
SÁBADOS 06:00-23:00 HORAS
DOMINGOS Y FESTIVOS 07:00-23:00 HORAS

RTP
LUNES A VIERNES 05:00-01:00 HORAS
SÁBADOS 05:00-01:00 HORAS
DOMINGOS Y FESTIVOS 05:30-00:00 HORAS

ECOBICI
TODOS LOS DÍAS 05:00-00:30 HORAS

TREN INTERURBANO
TODOS LOS DÍAS 06:00-21:30 HORAS

TREN SUBURBANO
LUNES A VIERNES 05:00-00:30 HORAS
SÁBADOS 06:00-00:30 HORAS
DOMINGOS Y FESTIVOS 07:00-00:30 HORAS

MEXIBÚS Y MEXICABLE

MEXIBÚS
LUNES A VIERNES 04:00-01:00 HORAS
SÁBADOS 04:00-01:00 HORAS
DOMINGOS Y FESTIVOS 04:30-01:00 HORAS

MEXICABLE
LUNES A VIERNES 05:00-23:30 HORAS
SÁBADOS 06:00-23:00 HORAS
DOMINGOS Y FESTIVOS 07:00-22:00 HORAS

Consulta los mapas de movilidad integrada de la Ciudad de México

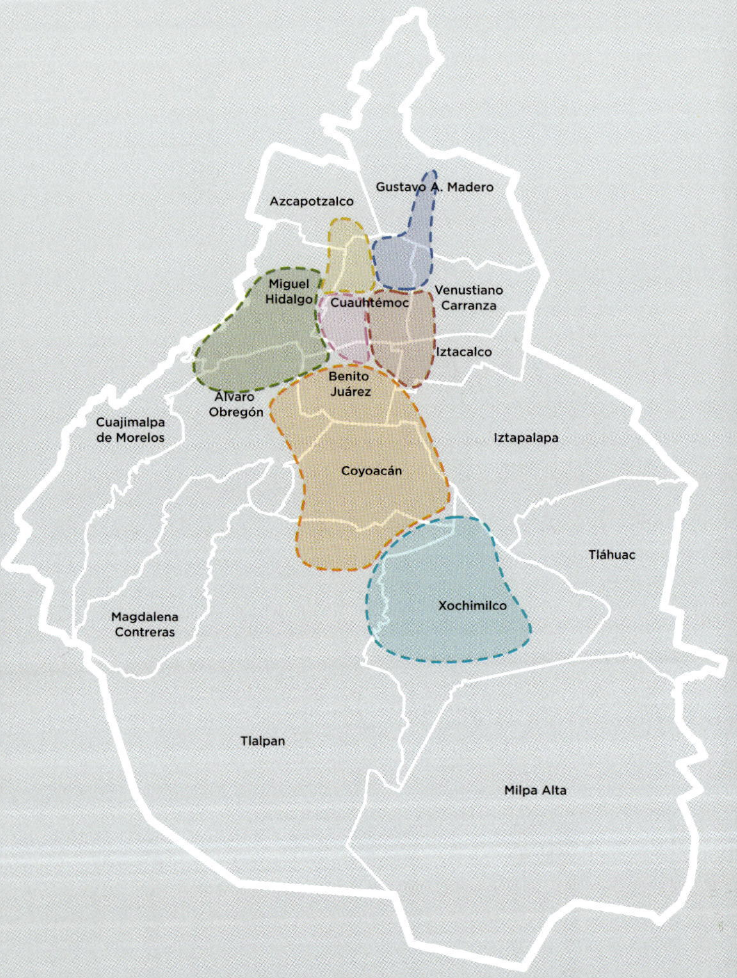

- **Route 1** | Centro Histórico
- **Route 2** | Catedral-Basílica
- **Route 3** | Bellas Artes-Garibaldi
- **Route 4** | Chapultepec
- **Route 5** | Zona Rosa
- **Route 6** | San Ángel-Estadio
- **Route 7** | Xochimilco

Credits

Photography

Ana Luz Valencia: pp. 23, 28, 30, 31, 32 (left), 33, 37, 40, 46-48, 49 (bottom), 57, 63, 65, 89, 104, 111, 116 (right), 117, 120, 122, 123, 135, 139 (left) 157, 159, 165, 169, 179, 191, 193, 197, 200, 207 (bottom), 208, 209, 214, 215

Andrea Griborio: p. 146

Andrés Semo: pp. 62, 131, 140, 149, 155, 158, 230, 231

Arturo Osorno (Cortesía Departamento de Proyectos Especiales UNAM): p. 173

Drkgk / Creative Commons CC0-1.0 Universal (https://es.wikipedia.org/wiki/Estaci%C3%B3n_Buenavista#/media/Archivo:Estaci%C3%B3n_Buenavista_CDMX.jpg): p. 98

D.R.© Luis Barragán / ProLitteris / SOMAAP / México / 2026 : p. 139 (right)

This creative work by DGE has been published first under a Creative Commons Creative Commons CC BY-SA 3.0 (https://mexicocity.cdmx.gob.mx/venues/metro-misterios/?lang=en): p. 77

Israyosoy S. (https://www.pexels.com/es-es/foto/el-iconico-angel-de-la-independencia-en-la-ciudad-de-mexico-28442669/): p. 154

Jaime Navarro: pp. 105, 190, 213

Jeffrey Greenberg/Universal Images Group via Getty Images Gettys: p. 25

José Ignacio Vargas: p. 141

Leonardo Perez Bautista/Creative Commons CC BY-SA 4.0 (https://es.wikipedia.org/wiki/Museo_Frida_Kahlo#/media/Archivo: Sala_1,_Museo_Frida_Kahlo.jpg): p. 183 (bottom)

Luis Young: p. 147

Matthias Bethke/Creative Commons CC BY-SA 4.0 (https://es.wikipedia.org/wiki/Museo_Frida_Kahlo#/media/Archivo:2006-08-20_Museo_Casa_Estudio_Diego_Rivera_y_Frida_Kahlo.jpg): p. 183 (top)

Moritz Bernoully: pp. 32 (right), 45, 70, 71, 74, 78, 79, 85, 87 (top), 96, 97, 99, 101, 108 (left), 109 (left), 116 (left), 127 (top), 128, 129, 132, 143, 161, 184, 196, 204, 205, 206 (top), 216, 217

Courtesy Museo Dolores Olmedo: pp. 222, 223

Nicuohulic (https://www.pexels.com/es-es/foto/arquitectura-monumento-piedra-exterior-11639097/): p. 102

Nin Solis: p. 99 (right)

Pablo Ramos: pp. 22, 24, 26, 27, 29, 34-36, 39, 41-44, 49 (top), 50-56, 64, 66-70, 72, 73, 75, 76, 84, 86, 87 (bottom), 88, 90-95, 100, 103, 106, 107, 108 (right), 109 (right), 110, 118, 119, 121, 124, 125 (bottom), 126, 127 (bottom), 130, 132-134, 136-138, 142, 144, 145, 156, 160, 162-164, 166, 167, 168, 170, 171, 172, 180-182, 185-189, 192, 194, 195, 198, 199, 201, 203, 211, 212, 224, 225-229, 232-235

Rafael Gamo: p. 210

Sandra Pereznieto: p. 148

Team730 Taller de Estudios y Análisis Metropolitanos: p. 38

This book was printed and bound in December 2025 by Offset Rebosán, in Mexico City. Typeface Inter designed by Rasmus Andersson was used. It was printed on 130g Couche paper. The total print run consists of 4,500 copies.